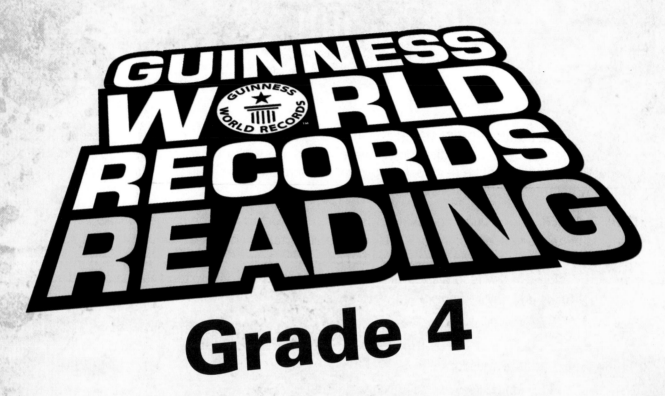

Grade 4

by Traci J. Bellas, Melissa & Henry Billings, Suzanne Francis, and Ashley Futrell Anderson

Carson-Dellosa Publishing LLC
Greensboro, North Carolina

GUINNESS WORLD RECORDS™ DISCLAIMER: Guinness World Records Limited has a very thorough accreditation system for records verification. However, while every effort is made to ensure accuracy, Guinness World Records Limited cannot be held responsible for any errors contained in this work. Feedback from our readers on any point of accuracy is always welcomed.

SAFETY DISCLAIMER: Attempting to break records or set new records can be dangerous. Appropriate advice should be taken first, and all record attempts are undertaken entirely at the participant's risk. In no circumstances will Guinness World Records Limited or Carson-Dellosa Publishing LLC have any liability for death or injury suffered in any record attempts. Guinness World Records Limited has complete discretion over whether or not to include any particular records in the annual Guinness World Records book.

Due to the publication date, the facts and the figures contained in this book are current as of July 2010.

Visit Guinness World Records at www.guinnessworldrecords.com.

Credits

Content Editor: Ginny Swinson

Copy Editor: Sandra Ogle

Layout and Cover Design: Van Harris

This book has been correlated to state, common core state, national, and Canadian provincial standards. Visit *www.carsondellosa.com* to search for and view its correlations to your standards.

Carson-Dellosa Publishing LLC
PO Box 35665
Greensboro, NC 27425 USA
www.carsondellosa.com

ISBN 978-1-936024-06-3
02-079121151

TABLE OF CONTENTS

INTRODUCTION

Guinness World Records™ Reading gives students the opportunity to shatter their own records—reading records, that is! Just as ordinary people can become Guinness World Record holders, students can become world record readers when they experience the excitement of *Guinness World Records™ Reading*. Designed for struggling or reluctant readers, students on grade level, and high achievers, *Guinness World Records™ Reading* helps improve reading comprehension skills and motivates students to do their best.

What does it mean to be the best? Guinness World Record holders know! Some of them are people, such as the woman who can scream louder than a jet engine. Some are animals, such as the greyhound that can jump over the heads of most people. Some record-holders are even vegetables and amusement parks! In this book, more than 50 stories chronicle the triumphs of people, animals, nature, science, and technology. The feats and successes are thrilling, and the records will amaze and inspire readers of all ages.

IN THIS BOOK

Guinness World Records™ Reading is divided into five themed units, with each unit highlighting incredible achievements in a specific category. Some of the records are exciting, some are unsettling, and some of them are just plain unbelievable—but, they are all extraordinary!

In the first unit, discover **Amazing Animals**, big and small: Meet a monkey you can hear four miles (6.4 km) away, a shrimp that can see a whopping 12 primary colors, and a dog with a mouth big enough to hold five tennis balls. You will even see a goat with horns that measure 52 inches (132 cm) from tip to tip. Who knew that you could fit a broom handle between a goat's horns?

In the next unit, explore records in **Engineering, Science & the Body**: Watch an earth-digging machine heavier than 6,000 cars, check out a man who can eat 200 earthworms in 30 seconds, and meet a boy who measured 7 feet (2.13 m) tall at age 12 and is still growing. Absolutely record breaking!

Experience the intensity of our home planet in **Earth Extremes**: Climb a ladder to see a sunflower taller than a two-story building, go into a hotel entirely made of ice (it melts away every year), and visit a plant that grew 2,563 cucumbers in one year. If that's not extreme, then what is?

Game Time! is sure to get you moving: Step into a tennis shoe that would fit someone 87 feet (27 m) tall, build a jigsaw puzzle with 21,600 pieces, and ride the longest true bicycle in the world. You'll be around the block before you know it!

Just when you think you have heard it all, **Wild, Wacky & Weird** proves you haven't: one record-breaker grew fingernails that are 32.3 feet (9.85 m) long, another raced furniture at a speed of 92 miles (148 km) per hour, and yet another covered himself with 613,500 bees! One woman even has a waist as small around as a mayonnaise jar. Weird? For sure!

HOW THIS BOOK WORKS

Guinness World Records™ Reading provides parents and teachers with materials and experiences that make reading compelling and fun for students. The high-interest, grade-level-appropriate reading passages are based on actual Guinness World Records. More than 50 short passages offer subject matter that motivates and engages even the most reluctant students to read, write, and explore fascinating topics. Students will become world record readers as they absorb astounding content, expand their vocabulary, and add to their knowledge of unusual facts and inspiring people.

Refer to each themed unit to select subjects of specific interest to your students or choose subjects based on units within your curriculum. Use the matrix to identify the skills that each lesson targets. Achievement of each skill varies, depending on the depth of knowledge students demonstrate in their answers.

- Each passage about a Guinness World Record holder is followed by questions that target such basic skills as recalling, summarizing, understanding the main idea, making connections, and drawing conclusions.

- Questions progress in difficulty using Bloom's Taxonomy for ease of differentiating instruction and for focused practice on higher-level thinking skills, such as predicting, applying, and analyzing.

- Vocabulary questions of various contexts and formats revisit challenging and practical vocabulary words (boldfaced in each passage) by working with words, definitions, and usage.

- Extension activities or critical response questions complete each question page. Students will expand their knowledge and creativity with more than 100 of these bonus questions to choose from!

- Summarizing puzzles and games at the end of each unit monitor student comprehension and reinforce vocabulary with an array of fun and engaging formats.

ARE *YOU* THE NEXT WORLD RECORD-HOLDER?

Do you think that you have what it takes to break a Guinness World Record? You just might! With dedication, persistence, and an idea, anything is possible. If you have an idea and you are ready to commit, get your family's permission and then go for it! Who knows? Your name could be in next year's record book. How do you do it? Read on!

First, what kind of record would you like to break? Do you have a unique talent? Are you the only person able to do something? If your talent is interesting or exciting and measurable, you have a good chance!

Do you own a unique object? Is it the only object of its kind? If it's a record that someone can break, such as owning the cow with the longest horns, then you're on your way. Or, if you think that you're the youngest person to achieve a certain feat, Guinness World Records may be interested. Just make sure that the feat is of international interest and, of course, something that is legal to do at your age!

Are you thinking of being the first at something? That's the hardest record to achieve. "Firsts" have to be important enough to have historical or international significance, such as the First Woman to Walk to the North Pole.

Not sure which record to break? Are you interested in going for a record that is regularly broken? The DJ marathon and various mass participation events are the records broken most often.

When you've decided which record to break, complete the registration form on the Guinness World Records Web site. Then, submit an application. Your application will include your proposal for the record. You'll know in about four weeks if your proposal is accepted. If it is, you are ready to go! Make sure that you follow the guidelines carefully. You'll have to collect and submit evidence of your record. Now, all you have to do is break that record!

Did You Know?

Guinness World Records receives more than 60,000 inquiries every year from potential record-breakers. A total of 40,000 records are in the Guinness database.

SKILLS MATRIX

Page Number	Comprehension Strategies								Vocabulary Development			Higher Order Thinking Skills					
	Recalling	Activating Prior Knowledge	Making Connections	Summarizing	Understanding Main Idea	Monitoring Comprehension	Drawing Conclusions	Determining Fact vs. Opinion	Increasing Vocabulary	Using Context Clues	Word Study	Predicting	Application	Analysis	Synthesis	Evaluation	Critical Response
11	✔	✔	✔	✔	✔	✔	✔		✔			✔	✔	✔			
13	✔	✔	✔			✔	✔		✔	✔			✔	✔			
15	✔	✔	✔	✔	✔	✔	✔		✔	✔		✔		✔			✔
17	✔	✔	✔		✔	✔			✔	✔			✔	✔			
19	✔		✔	✔	✔	✔			✔	✔		✔	✔	✔			
21	✔	✔	✔			✔			✔	✔			✔	✔	✔	✔	
23	✔	✔				✔	✔		✔	✔			✔	✔	✔		
25	✔	✔	✔	✔	✔	✔			✔	✔	✔	✔	✔	✔			
27	✔	✔	✔			✔			✔	✔			✔	✔			
29	✔	✔		✔	✔	✔			✔	✔			✔				
31	✔	✔	✔		✔	✔			✔	✔			✔	✔			
33	✔	✔	✔	✔	✔	✔	✔		✔	✔			✔	✔		✔	
34	✔					✔											
35	✔					✔			✔	✔							
37	✔	✔	✔		✔	✔	✔		✔	✔		✔		✔		✔	✔
39	✔	✔	✔			✔			✔	✔			✔	✔		✔	
41	✔	✔			✔	✔			✔	✔	✔		✔	✔			
43	✔	✔				✔		✔	✔	✔		✔	✔	✔		✔	✔
45	✔	✔			✔	✔			✔	✔		✔	✔	✔		✔	
47	✔	✔	✔		✔			✔	✔	✔	✔	✔	✔	✔			
49	✔		✔		✔	✔		✔	✔	✔		✔	✔	✔	✔		
51	✔		✔		✔	✔			✔	✔		✔	✔	✔		✔	
53	✔	✔	✔		✔	✔	✔		✔	✔				✔		✔	
54	✔		✔		✔	✔											
55	✔					✔			✔	✔							
57	✔	✔	✔	✔	✔	✔			✔	✔		✔	✔	✔			
59	✔	✔	✔		✔	✔			✔	✔			✔	✔			
61	✔		✔			✔			✔	✔					✔		
63	✔	✔	✔	✔		✔		✔	✔	✔			✔	✔			
65	✔		✔			✔	✔		✔	✔			✔	✔			
67	✔	✔	✔			✔			✔	✔	✔	✔	✔	✔			
69	✔	✔	✔		✔	✔	✔		✔	✔		✔	✔	✔	✔		

Page Number	Comprehension Strategies								Vocabulary Development			Higher Order Thinking Skills					
	Recalling	Activating Prior Knowledge	Making Connections	Summarizing	Understanding Main Idea	Monitoring Comprehension	Drawing Conclusions	Determining Fact vs. Opinion	Increasing Vocabulary	Using Context Clues	Word Study	Predicting	Application	Analysis	Synthesis	Evaluation	Critical Response
71	✔	✔	✔		✔				✔	✔		✔	✔	✔			
73	✔	✔				✔	✔		✔	✔		✔					✔
75	✔	✔				✔			✔	✔			✔	✔	✔		
76	✔					✔				✔							
77	✔								✔								
79	✔	✔	✔		✔	✔	✔		✔				✔	✔			
81	✔	✔	✔		✔				✔	✔		✔		✔	✔		
83	✔	✔	✔	✔		✔	✔		✔	✔				✔			
85	✔	✔	✔	✔	✔	✔		✔	✔	✔		✔	✔	✔			
87	✔	✔	✔			✔	✔		✔	✔		✔	✔	✔			
89	✔		✔			✔			✔	✔		✔					✔
91	✔		✔	✔	✔	✔			✔	✔			✔	✔	✔		
93	✔	✔	✔			✔		✔	✔		✔	✔	✔	✔	✔		
95	✔	✔	✔		✔	✔	✔	✔	✔	✔		✔	✔	✔			
97	✔	✔	✔			✔			✔	✔	✔		✔	✔			
99	✔	✔	✔			✔			✔	✔			✔	✔			
101	✔		✔	✔	✔		✔		✔	✔	✔		✔	✔	✔		
102	✔		✔		✔	✔											
103									✔								
105	✔	✔	✔	✔		✔	✔	✔	✔	✔		✔		✔			
107	✔	✔	✔			✔	✔	✔	✔		✔		✔	✔			
109	✔	✔	✔			✔	✔	✔	✔	✔		✔	✔				
111	✔	✔	✔	✔	✔	✔	✔		✔				✔	✔	✔	✔	
113	✔	✔	✔	✔	✔			✔	✔	✔		✔					
115	✔	✔			✔	✔		✔	✔		✔	✔					✔
117	✔	✔	✔	✔	✔		✔		✔	✔	✔	✔	✔	✔	✔		
119	✔	✔	✔		✔	✔			✔	✔			✔	✔	✔		
121	✔					✔	✔	✔	✔	✔		✔	✔	✔			
123	✔	✔	✔	✔	✔	✔		✔	✔	✔	✔		✔	✔			
124									✔								
125	✔		✔			✔											

BALLOON-POPPING DOG!

On TV

■ Read the passage.
Fastest Time to Pop 100 Balloons by a Dog, February 24, 2008

Some dogs do not like loud noises, like popping a balloon. But, Anastasia just loves that sound! Her owner first noticed Anastasia's special talent at a New Year's Eve party. When all of the balloons appeared, Anastasia thought it was a game. She wanted to pop as many as she could. Now, she holds the world record!

Her first balloon contest in 2005 involved **helium** balloons. Anastasia, a Jack Russell terrier, was one of 10 finalists in that contest. Now, she bites standard party balloons attached to the ground. Each one is inflated with air and measures 8 inches (20.3 cm) across. Her world record is 100 popped balloons in 44.49 seconds.

Anastasia appeared on TV in dog food and department store commercials before her record-breaking days. Since then, she has shown her skills on several TV shows. In fact, Anastasia actually broke her old world record of 53.7 seconds on a national morning TV show. Her trainer said that Anastasia really gets excited when a blimp flies over the backyard!

DID YOU KNOW?
Jack Russell terriers are intelligent, athletic, and fearless dogs. They are known to bark loudly and were first used to hunt out foxes, badgers, and groundhogs. Jack Russell terriers are fun-loving dogs that can entertain themselves.

Name_____ Date_____

■ Answer the questions.

1. Anastasia's owner discovered that her dog had a special talent at a

_____

2. Anastasia pops balloons by
   A. sitting on them.
   B. using her toenails.
   C. biting them.

3. What kinds of TV experiences has Anastasia had?

   _____

   _____

   _____

4. What characteristics of Jack Russell terriers might
   make them good balloon poppers?

   _____

   _____

5. Why might **helium**-filled balloons be more difficult to use when breaking a world record?

   _____

   _____

   _____

6. Why do you think Anastasia gets excited when a blimp flies by?

   _____

   _____

■ Choose one extension activity.

A. Write three questions that you would like to ask Anastasia's trainer. Then, write
   what you think her answers might be.
B. Anastasia is a famous record-breaking dog. Find articles about other famous
   dogs in history.

DRAGONS: FACT, NOT FICTION

■ Read the passage.

Largest Lizard

When you hear of dragons, you may think of fictional tales about beasts that breathe fire. But, did you know that a lizard called a Komodo dragon exists that is just as fierce? Komodo dragons are also called Komodo monitors or ora. They live on the southeastern islands of Indonesia. By weight, Komodo dragons are the world's Largest Lizards. These lizards have been alive for millions of years, but their existence has been a mystery until about 100 years ago.

> ### DID YOU KNOW?
> The saliva in the Komodo dragon's mouth has over 50 kinds of bacteria. Most animals that escape die of blood poisoning within 24 hours of the bite. Scientists are studying this saliva to see if it can help control diseases in the future.

The Komodo's teeth are often compared to those of a shark. A Komodo has about 60 teeth, which are broken and replaced frequently. This keeps the teeth sharp enough to cut chunks out of its prey. The dragons use their **sharp** sense of smell to find prey. These fast-moving animals can climb trees and swim to catch something to eat.

Komodo dragons also are **scavengers** and eat the bodies of dead animals. They can eat up to 80 percent of their body weight in one meal. If you weighed 100 pounds (45.4 kg), that would mean you would have to eat an 80-pound (36-kg) hamburger to keep up with this dragon!

Name_____ Date_____

■ Answer the questions.

1. Komodo dragons are also known by what two names?

_____

2. Circle *T* for true or *F* for false.

A. People have known about Komodo dragons for millions of years. **T** **F**

B. A Komodo dragon's saliva contains no bacteria. **T** **F**

3. In what way are Komodo dragons and sharks alike?
   A. They can both climb trees.
   B. They both use gills to breathe.
   C. They both have teeth that are replaced often.

4. Which definition best describes **sharp** as it is used in "their sharp sense of smell"?
   A. pointed
   B. strong
   C. sudden

5. Name other animals that are examples of **scavengers**.

_____

_____

6. From this passage, you can conclude that Komodo dragons are
   A. dangerous animals.
   B. slow, lazy creatures.
   C. related to dinosaurs.

■ Choose one extension activity.

A. Research dragons from various legends. Compare and contrast them with Komodo dragons. Create a poster to display your information.

B. Show the length of a Komodo dragon on a chart. Research other animals of interest and graph their measurements on the chart as a comparison.

MONKEY RISE AND SHINE

■ Read the passage.
Noisiest Land Animal

Animals that live in the rain forests of Latin America have their own special alarm clocks—howler monkeys! These monkeys make loud, wailing noises at dawn and dusk each day. Their howls can be heard three to four miles (4.8–6.4 km) into the forest. Howler monkeys are so loud that they have been named the world's Noisiest Land Animals.

Male howler monkeys are black. Females are brown. As adults, both male and female weigh about 15 pounds (6.8 kg). Both grow to be about two feet (62 cm) long. This does not include their 30-inch (76-cm) **prehensile** tail. A prehensile tail is often used for grabbing things and commonly used for balance. Howlers use this amazing tail like an extra arm to hang from tree branches.

Because howler monkeys are **herbivores**, their diet includes mostly leaves, fruit, and flowers. Except for sloths, howler monkeys are the slowest mammals in the rain forest. They spend about 15 hours of their day asleep. They prefer to stay in their small communities, living in particular areas of the forest. This makes their habitat at risk for destruction. Howler monkeys also are hunted for food by local tribes. Some even are exported as pets. But, they make terrible pets! Scientists are concerned that, without more awareness, howler monkeys will become extinct during our lifetime.

Name_____ Date_____

■ **Answer the questions.**

1. How far can the calls of howler monkeys be heard?

_____

2. What is a **prehensile** tail? Can you name other animals with prehensile tails?

_____

_____

3. How would you compare the male and female howler monkeys?
    A. Both are the same color, size, and weight.
    B. Both are the same color and size but different weight.
    C. Both are the same size and weight but different colors.

4. Howler monkeys are **herbivores**. What does this mean? What other animals do you know that are herbivores?

_____

_____

5. Which facts from the passage support the author's statement that howler monkeys "make terrible pets"?

_____

_____

6. Predict what you think would happen if troops of howler monkeys shared the same territory.

_____

_____

■ **Choose one statement. Then, explain why you agree or disagree.**
    A. Exotic animals should not be sold as pets.
    B. Local tribes should not be allowed to hunt howler monkeys.

NEPTUNE'S TINY HERD

■ Read the passage.
Slowest Fish

Mysterious sea creatures have always captured people's imaginations. Children's books are full of stories about mermaids and sea horses. Unlike mermaids, however, sea horses are real. Sea horses may have heads like horses, but they also have front pouches like kangaroos and tails like monkeys. They aren't really horses at all. Sea horses actually are extremely unusual fish.

More than 30 different kinds of sea horses exist. They live in warm ocean waters all over the world. They can range in size from one-fourth of an inch (0.6 cm) to one foot (30 cm) long. Sea horses come in many colors. Some even use **camouflage** to hide from their enemies.

Sea horses are unusual because they mate for life. They are one of few fish species in which the male gives birth to the young. Male sea horses carry their babies in kangaroo-like pouches on their bellies. Babies are born as fully formed tiny sea horses. They immediately begin swimming in the ocean.

Due to their body structure, sea horses swim upright. This makes them the Slowest Fish in the ocean. They cannot swim fast because they have only their **dorsal** fins on their backs to move them forward. This fin can only flutter about 35 times per second. A sea horse uses the two smaller fins on either side of its head to steer. These are called pectoral fins. They use their prehensile tails to hold on to coral or seaweed. This prevents them from being swept away by ocean currents. Their long snouts suck in plankton like a straw.

DID YOU KNOW?
In ancient Rome, many believed Neptune, the god of the ocean, used large sea horses to pull his chariot. When fishermen saw the tiny creatures in the sea, they were fascinated by them. They thought that these fish were related to Neptune's horses.

Name_____ Date_____

■ Answer the questions.

1. Circle *T* for true or *F* for false.

    A. Mermaids are real creatures.   **T**   **F**

    B. A sea horse uses its snout like a straw to suck in plankton.   **T**   **F**

2. About how many varieties of sea horses exist?

    A. 50

    B. 25

    C. 30

3. An animal that uses **camouflage** for defense

    A. hides behind large objects.

    B. blends in with its surroundings.

    C. shows its teeth or claws.

4. Identify one way that sea horses are like other fish.

_____

_____

5. The author describes sea horses as "unusual." In what ways are sea horses unusual?

_____

_____

6. What is the difference between **dorsal** fins and pectoral fins?

_____

_____

■ Choose one extension activity.

A. Design a machine that could help sea horses swim faster. Share your invention with your classmates.

B. Research the different types of sea horses and the oceans in which they live. Create a map that displays the location of each species.

LEFT IN THE LURCH

■ Read the passage.

Largest Horn Circumference—Steer, May 6, 2003

If you like animals, you may find Gassville, Arkansas, an exciting place to visit. It is the home of Janice Wolf and Rocky Ridge Animal Refuge. Wolf has turned her home into a **shelter** for abused and abandoned animals. She cares for dogs, cats, geese, and donkeys. She also has other animals like a zebra, deer, and water buffalo. But, Wolf's most famous resident of all time was Lurch, the Watusi steer.

> **DID YOU KNOW?**
> **Circumference** is the distance around any circle or curvy shape. This measurement is usually used in geometry to measure the distance around the outside of a cylinder or a circle.

Watusi cattle come from Africa. But, Lurch was born on October 11, 1995, on a farm in Missouri. Wolf adopted Lurch when he was five weeks old. As Lurch grew, Wolf noticed that his horns were unusually large. Watusi steer are known for their large horns. The horns of other cattle grow in length. But, the horns of Watusi cattle grow in **circumference**. Lurch set a Guinness World Records™ record for having the Largest Horn Circumference. His horns measured 37.5 inches (95.2 cm) around.

Lurch spent his days on the refuge watching as carloads of people came to visit. People from all around the world came to see Lurch. He has even appeared on TV!

■ **Answer the questions.**

1. Why would people who like animals want to visit Gassville, Arkansas?
    A. They could meet people from Africa.
    B. They could visit an animal refuge with many different kinds of animals.
    C. They could be on TV.

2. Where do Watusi steer usually come from?

_____

_____

3. Janice Wolf has turned her home into a **shelter** for abused and abandoned animals. Which statement explains what Wolf has done to her home?
    A. She has created a safe place for animals to live.
    B. She has built a tent to keep out the rain.
    C. She has given people who need food and a place to stay someplace to live.

4. As Lurch grew, what was different about him? What did Wolf notice?

_____

_____

5. What other animals are in the Rocky Ridge Animal Refuge?

_____

_____

■ **Choose one extension activity.**

    A. Imagine that you are interviewing Janice Wolf. Write a list of questions that you would ask.
    B. Research the job of veterinarian. What education or training is needed to become a veterinarian? What kind of person would be a good veterinarian? Create a job posting for a veterinarian to care for the animals at Rocky Ridge Animal Refuge.

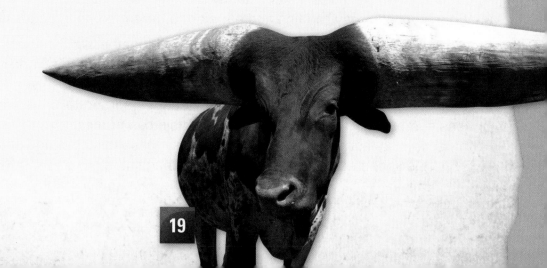

A NOSE THAT KNOWS

■ Read the passage.
Fastest Eater (Mammals)

The star-nosed mole may be the strangest animal that you have ever seen. But, it is also the fastest-eating mammal in the world! Star-nosed moles live underground in wet, wooded areas or swamps. Their narrow, underground tunnels are in complete darkness, so their eyes do not develop very well. This means that they are practically blind. They depend on their strange noses for almost everything!

This unusual nose has 22 tentacle-like fingers that look like a pink sea anemone. Moles use their **unique** noses to find prey and find their way in the dark. When these moles look for food, their nose tentacles are constantly moving. They can touch 13 areas of the ground in just one second. They can find and eat eight different items in under two seconds!

When a mole eats, the tentacles are clumped together and stay out of the way. Moles feed on earthworms, insects, and mollusks. When these moles find something in their way, they use their noses to decide if it is something to eat. The nose sends important information to the brain. This information then gets sorted. The sorting tells the mole whether a smell means something good to eat. The mole's brain can **process** this information in less than a second! It is so fast that the mole sometimes makes mistakes and passes by food. But, don't worry! This speed eater turns around and tries again!

■ Answer the questions.

1. Which is a true statement?

    A. The star-nosed mole is the slowest animal in the world.

    B. The star-nosed mole only eats plants.

    C. The star-nosed mole is the fastest-eating mammal in the world.

2. Why are star-nosed moles practically blind?

_____

_____

3. The author compares the nose of the star-nosed mole to a pink sea anemone. To what would you compare the mole's nose?

_____

_____

4. Which word best describes **unique** as it is used in this passage?

    A. special

    B. large

    C. common

5. Contrast the tentacles on the mole's nose when it is looking for food and when it eats.

_____

_____

6. Which phrase best describes **process** as it is used in this passage?

    A. delete information

    B. change information from one form to another

    C. turn raw ingredients into food

■ Choose one extension activity.

A. Try a race of your own. Put a variety of items on a tray and blindfold yourself. Have a teacher or classmate time you to see how long it takes you to select each item individually. Take turns with classmates. Make a graph to show the results.

B. Louis Braille was a blind man who developed a way for the blind to read. Research Mr. Braille and create a poster showing his unique alphabet. Try writing your name using his alphabet.

AMAZING EYESIGHT

■ Read the passage.
Greatest Color Vision

Humans see only three **primary** colors of light: red, green, and blue. Some animals see more colors than humans. Most animals see fewer colors than humans. In fact, some animals can see only black and white. The mantis shrimp holds the record for seeing the most visible colors. It can see 11 or 12 primary colors of light. It sees colors that are invisible to humans and other animals.

The mantis shrimp is not actually a shrimp, but it looks like one. It is a **crustacean** that is a distant relative of the lobster. Mantis shrimp live in the shallow waters of tropical coral reefs. Scientists are not sure why they can see so many colors. Some believe that it may be because of their environment. Most plants and animals around mantis shrimp are very colorful.

It is important for a mantis shrimp to be able to quickly see its predators and its prey. In fact, some of the animals that it likes to eat are almost invisible to most other animals. But, the mantis shrimp can see them clearly!

DID YOU KNOW?

Mantis shrimp are forceful. They have the fastest recorded attack of any known animal. Some mantis shrimp smash the shells of their food with their front legs. Others spear food with sharp claws. When scientists first tried to film a mantis shrimp's attack, their cameras were not fast enough to capture the strike. Some people keep mantis shrimp in aquariums. However, they have been known to break the glass walls of their tanks with their powerful front legs.

■ **Answer the questions.**

1. The mantis shrimp can see _____ **primary** colors of light. Humans can

    see only _____ primary colors of light.

2. What is one possible reason that mantis shrimp can see so many colors?

    _____

    _____

3. Which animal is not a **crustacean**?

    A. lobster

    B. parrot

    C. mantis shrimp

4. Why is it important for the mantis shrimp to be able to see predators?

    _____

    _____

5. Circle *T* for true or *F* for false.

    A. Some animals see only black and white.   T   F

    B. Some mantis shrimp can break the glass wall of an aquarium.   T   F

■ **Choose one extension activity.**

   A. Imagine that you have mantis shrimp in your aquarium. Find information about how to
   care for mantis shrimp. Write directions for your friend who will care for them while you
   are on vacation.

   B. Why do you think some animals see differently or better than other animals?

FETCHING FRIENDS

■ Read the passage.
Most Tennis Balls Held in the Mouth—Dog, July 6, 2003

Many pet owners have played fetch with their dogs. This is a simple game where the owner throws a ball and the dog brings it back. It is a favorite among many dogs. But, only a few dogs have a claim to fame for playing fetch. Augie, a golden retriever, holds the Guinness World Records™ record for playing this game. His talent is being able to collect and hold five tennis balls in his mouth at the same time.

Golden retrievers originally came from Scotland where they were used as companions for hunters. They helped hunters find birds or other small **game** that had been caught. These dogs became known as retrievers because they brought back or retrieved what hunters had caught. This ability makes them not only excellent guides but also great search and rescue dogs.

The golden retriever is one of the most popular dog breeds in the United States. Golden retrievers are known for being loyal, intelligent, and friendly. They are also very alert and trustworthy. They have a strong desire to please their owners. Golden retrievers are good family dogs too. They are patient and gentle with children. Because they are people lovers, they need a lot of attention.

The average size of golden retrievers is 55 to 75 pounds (25–34 kg). Their coats have two layers. The top layer is soft and wavy. It sheds to keep the dog comfortable during any season. The bottom layer **repels** water easily. This is important because golden retrievers like to swim. Golden retrievers are active dogs. This means that they need exercise every day. It is an important part of their care. Interesting types of activities keep golden retrievers happy, especially when the activity involves playing fetch with a friend!

Name_____ Date_____

■ Answer the questions.

1. Which best describes the game of fetch?
   - **A.** Someone hits a ball with a stick, and a dog catches it.
   - **B.** Someone gives a dog a ball, and the dog hides it.
   - **C.** Someone throws a ball, and a dog brings it back.

2. Where did golden retrievers originally come from?
   - **A.** Dallas, Texas
   - **B.** Scotland
   - **C.** the United States

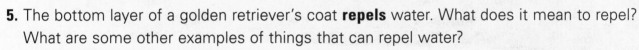

3. Which is <u>not</u> an example of **game** as it is used in the passage?
   - **A.** basketball
   - **B.** rabbit
   - **C.** squirrels

4. How did golden retrievers get their name?

   _____

   _____

5. The bottom layer of a golden retriever's coat **repels** water. What does it mean to repel? What are some other examples of things that can repel water?

   _____

   _____

6. Based on the information from this passage, would a golden retriever be a good pet for you? Why or why not?

   _____

   _____

■ Choose one extension activity.

A. Golden retrievers need a lot of exercise. Design an exercise schedule to use with a golden retriever for one week. Be sure to include some interesting and fun activities.

B. Caring for a dog is a great responsibility. Research puppy and dog care. Create a brochure for new dog owners that will help them care for their new friend.

ONE SMALL SERPENT

■ Read the passage.
Smallest Species of Rattlesnake

Have you gone for a walk in the woods recently? If so, a chance exists that you were walking through the **habitat** of a pigmy rattlesnake. Pigmy rattlesnakes are the world's Smallest Species of Rattlesnake.

Because of their size, pigmy rattlesnakes can be hard to see. Adult snakes are only about 18 inches (46 cm) long. When these snakes are coiled, they are about the size of a pinecone. These snakes can be dangerous because they are so well camouflaged. This means that they can blend in with their surroundings. Pigmy rattlesnakes vary in color, but most are tan, gray, or reddish.

Pigmy rattlesnakes feed on lizards, mice, frogs, and other small snakes and mammals. They are aggressive snakes and will strike if bothered. The **venom** from this strike is what kills the pigmy snake's prey. Scientists are studying this venom for use in medicines to help prevent heart disease.

DID YOU KNOW?

Pigmy rattlesnakes, also known as ground rattlers, belong to a group of venomous snakes called pit vipers. This group includes all of the Southeast United States' venomous snakes *except* coral snakes. Pit vipers get their name because they have special heat-sensing organs. These organs are located between their eyes and nostrils and are known as "pits." These pits help direct the snake's strike toward its prey.

Name _____ Date _____

■ Answer the questions.

1. Circle *T* for true or *F* for false.

    A. Pigmy rattlesnakes are venomous snakes.   **T**   **F**

    B. Pit vipers have heat-sensing organs between their
        eyes and nostrils.   **T**   **F**

2. Which place is an example of the pigmy rattlesnakes' natural **habitat**?

    A. a cage in a zoo

    B. a desert

    C. a wooded area

3. What are some animal habitats in your area? How do they compare with the habitat of the pigmy rattlesnake?

_____

_____

4. Which statement does <u>not</u> explain why pigmy rattlesnakes are dangerous?

    A. Pigmy rattlesnakes are different colors.

    B. Pigmy rattlesnakes use camouflage to hide from their prey.

    C. Pigmy rattlesnakes are small and difficult to see.

5. Which best describes the meaning of **venom**?

    A. a loud sound

    B. poison

    C. spray

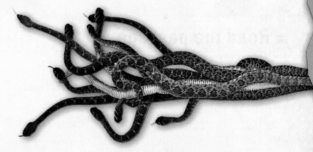

■ Choose one extension activity.

A. The author writes that scientists are studying the venom of pigmy rattlesnakes for use in medicines. Research other animals whose venoms are being studied to help in the medical field.

B. Discover more information about the habitats of animals in your area. Choose one animal and build a model of its habitat.

CREEPY CRAWLER

■ Read the passage.
Largest Spider, April 1965

Many people are afraid of spiders. If you are one of those people, this spider might give you the creeps! The Goliath bird-eating spider is the world's Largest Spider! The largest spider was found in 1965 on an expedition in Venezuela. With a leg span of 11 inches (28 cm), it was about the size of a dinner plate. Goliath spiders are members of the tarantula family and are **native** to South America.

> **DID YOU KNOW?**
> Some people in South America collect and eat Goliath bird-eating spiders. They are cooked over an open fire and eaten like crabs. The fangs are used as toothpicks.

Dr. Robert Bustard raises spiders. He has more than 2,000 tarantulas. He also raises crickets to feed his hungry spiders. Dr. Bustard is the proud owner of a Goliath spider. His two-year-old tarantula is a record-setting example. It weighs 6 ounces (170 g), which is about as much as a cup of yogurt.

The most dangerous thing about Goliath spiders is their ability to release irritating hairs from their bodies. These hairs can irritate skin and eyes.

Another interesting quality of Goliath spiders is their ability to make noise. They rub their legs together to make a hissing sound. This rubbing can be heard up to 15 feet (4.6 m) away. The spider makes this noise when it feels **threatened**. Although its name suggests it is a bird-eater, this spider rarely eats birds. It prefers frogs, insects, lizards, snakes, and even bats.

■ Answer the questions.

1. This spider is a member of the _____ family.

2. Goliath bird-eating spiders are native to South America. What does it mean to be **native** to a place? To what place are you native?

_____

_____

3. For what is Dr. Robert Bustard famous?
    A. He raises crickets.
    B. He owns 20,000 tarantulas.
    C. He is the owner of a prize-winning Goliath bird-eating spider.

4. What is the most dangerous thing about these spiders?
    A. their hairs
    B. their size
    C. their bite

5. Goliath bird-eating spiders make noise by rubbing their legs together. What other animals rub their legs together to make noise?

_____

_____

6. When a giant spider feels threatened, it makes noises to defend itself. Which word best describes **threatened**?
    A. angry
    B. afraid
    C. sad

■ Choose one extension activity.

A. Some people keep tarantulas as pets. Research the care of pet tarantulas. Create an advertisement that shares your information and persuades someone to choose a tarantula as a pet.

B. The Goliath bird-eating spider lives in the rain forests of South America. What other animals live in the rain forests? Investigate the various animals and create a poster about your favorite.

SOARING CINDY

■ Read the passage.
Highest Jump by a Dog, October 7, 2006

Soaring Cindy holds the Guinness World Records™ record for the Highest Jump by a Dog. Cindy's full name is Cinderella May a Holly Grey, and she is a greyhound. With such a long name, it is no wonder that people nicknamed her Soaring Cindy. Others call her Cindy.

Cindy was born in Florida. At first, no one wanted this dog. Cindy seemed to have too much energy for many people. Fortunately, Kathy Conroy and Kate Long came along. They already had a two-year-old dog named Colleen. They wanted a second dog to keep Colleen company. Cindy was the perfect choice.

"To soar" means to fly high into the air, so it is exactly the right nickname for this dog. Cindy's winning jump was 5 feet 8 inches (172.7 cm). Some people are surprised that a greyhound holds the record for Highest Jump by a Dog. People think of greyhounds as being fast, not bouncy. Greyhounds certainly are fast. They can run up to 45 miles (72 km) per hour.

Greyhounds are unique in other ways. They have great eyesight. They can see things up to one-half mile (0.8 km) away. Also, they have no layer of fat on their body. This means that they are **sensitive** to the cold. If they are out in snow or rain, they can get chilly. If you see a greyhound wearing a sweater, the owner is not being silly. He or she is being a responsible pet owner.

■ Answer the questions.

1. Circle *T* for true or *F* for false.

    A. Greyhounds can run 72 miles (116 km) per hour.   **T**   **F**

    B. Greyhounds have poor eyesight.   **T**   **F**

2. Kathy Conroy and Kate Long took in Cindy because
    A. they wanted company for their other dog.
    B. they thought that she could be a record-setting jumper.
    C. they wanted a dog without much energy.

3. What does **sensitive** mean in this passage? Are you sensitive to the cold? Explain.

_____

_____

4. Why do you think the author says "it is no wonder" people call Cindy by a nickname?

_____

_____

5. In what ways would you enjoy having a dog that could jump really high? In what ways might that be a problem?

_____

_____

■ Choose one extension activity.

A. Gather information about greyhounds. Then, write a paragraph telling what you have learned, including at least three new facts.

B. Soaring Cindy is an amazing jumper. What other animals are great jumpers? Choose one to research. Prepare a short presentation for your classmates.

A GOAT NAMED UNCLE SAM

■ Read the passage.
Longest Domestic Goat Horns, April 16, 2004

Bill Wentling's goat has an unusual name—Uncle Sam. Uncle Sam had extremely long horns, but Wentling didn't think much about it. Then one day, a boy showed him the Guinness World Records™ record for the Longest Domestic Goat Horns. "Uncle Sam could beat that," Wentling thought.

Uncle Sam's horns beat the old record by 9 inches (24 cm). It was the first time an American goat had held the title. From one tip to the other, Uncle Sam's horns measured 52 inches (132 cm).

DID YOU KNOW?
For hundreds of years, many useful items have been made from goat horns. Goat horns have been used to make the heads of canes and walking sticks. They also have been used to make buttons and combs.

Reporters asked why Uncle Sam's horns grew so long. Wentling said that he had no idea. According to him, the goat had "a normal diet of basic feed and grass."

In 2005, Uncle Sam died from cancer at age nine. Wentling arranged to have him stuffed and mounted, with his horns **intact**. Wentling had hoped to keep the stuffed goat at home, but his wife did not like that idea. Instead, Wentling had him placed in the lobby of a local restaurant. This turned out to be a good choice. "I thought it might be nice if Uncle Sam were displayed somewhere that people could see him," explained Wentling. The stuffed version of Uncle Sam is in the lobby of the Brownstown Restaurant in Brownstown, Pennsylvania.

Name_____ Date_____

■ **Answer the questions.**

1. Circle *T* for true or *F* for false.

A. Uncle Sam was the first American goat to hold the title for
Longest Domestic Goat Horns.   **T**   **F**

B. Placing the stuffed goat in a restaurant lobby was a bad choice.   **T**   **F**

2. What made Bill Wentling decide to have his goat's horns measured for Guinness
World Records?

_____

_____

3. What is the definition of **intact** in the passage?
A. not easily seen
B. not removed
C. not smooth

4. Do you think that a goat's diet determines how big his horns grow? Why or why not?

_____

_____

5. What two comments from Wentling indicate that he was proud of Uncle Sam?

_____

_____

6. Do you think that Uncle Sam is a good name for a goat? Why or why not?

_____

_____

■ **Choose one extension activity.**

A. Write a dialogue between Bill Wentling and his wife. Imagine that
he is trying to convince her to keep the stuffed goat in
their house and that she is resisting.

B. Write a paragraph to go on the back of the
menu at the Brownstown Restaurant. The
paragraph should explain to diners why a
stuffed goat is in the lobby.

REVIEW: AMAZING ANIMALS

■ **Complete the passage by writing the correct word in each blank.**

Animals do truly amazing things! Some are trained to accomplish remarkable tasks. Others

come by their talent naturally. Anastasia first revealed her talent to her owner at a party

when she began to pop every _____ in sight! Another dog, Augie, also holds a
         (1)

record. He can hold five _____ _____ in his mouth at one time!
      (2)   (3)

If you think Augie has a big mouth, then you probably haven't been in the jungle lately. It's

no wonder that the noisiest land animal is called a _____ monkey, especially
             (4)

when you consider that he can be heard four miles (6.4 km) away!

Then, there's an animal that's known for what it *doesn't* do. In fact, the

_____ _____ doesn't move very fast at all. It is the slowest fish
 (5)   (6)

in the sea. But, when it comes to moving quickly, no one can beat the _____
               (7)

_____. These strange-looking creatures can gulp down eight different items
 (8)

in less than two seconds! While we're near water, let's look at an animal that can see a lot

better than we can. _____ _____ can see a whopping 11 or
     (9)   (10)

12 primary colors compared to the three humans can see.

Some animals are large by nature. The fierce Komodo dragon is the largest type of

_____ in the world. And talk about large, Lurch holds the record for the largest
 (11)

horn circumference of any _____. People were sure to "steer" clear of him!
        (12)

But, scary or dangerous doesn't always have four legs. Sometimes, it's a dinner-plate-

sized spider, like the _____ _____ spider. And sometimes, it's a
     (13)   (14)

small but definitely venomous snake, like the tiny _____ _____.
           (15)   (16)

All of these animals have one thing in common. They may have been swimming, creeping,

crawling, jumping, or just growing, but they all became world record-breakers!

REVIEW: AMAZING ANIMALS

■ **Use the clues to complete the puzzle.**

| camouflage | habitat | herbivores | process | scavengers | venom |
| crustacean | helium | primary | repel | unique | |

ACROSS

1. To _____ information is to change it from one form to another.

3. This type of gas makes a balloon float.

7. A natural home for an animal or a plant is its _____ .

8. A bite from a snake might inject you with this.

9. If something is one-of-a-kind, it is _____ .

10. To _____ something means to resist it or drive it away.

DOWN

2. A shellfish is one.

3. These types of animals eat leaves, fruit, and flowers.

4. A _____ color is a basic color that can be used to make other colors.

5. These types of animals eat dead animals.

6. This protective coloring helps animals blend in with their surroundings.

MEET THE WORLD'S HAIRIEST FAMILY

■ Read the passage.

Hairiest Family

Danny Ramos Gomez (Mexico) has a rare condition. It is called hypertrichosis. This condition causes hair to grow all over the body. In fact, it produces hair on 98 percent of the body. This condition has been passed down through Danny's family for five generations—19 members of his family have had it. This condition has earned them the title of Hairiest Family in the world.

Women in Danny's family have had a light-to-medium coat of hair. The men have had even thicker hair. Only their hands and feet have stayed relatively hairless. Danny's brother, Larry, has the condition. As small boys, he and Danny were not treated well. They were put on display. People called them "wolf children" and paid money to see them.

Fortunately, this grim life did not continue. The boys were rescued by a circus owner. His name was Mundo Campo. He trained the boys to be acrobats at the Mexican National Circus. In time, Danny and Larry became stars of the circus.

At one point, the brothers were offered a chance to act on a TV show. It was a popular science-fiction show. They turned down the offer. "We don't want to be seen as aliens," Danny explained. "We have learned that people who are different can still have **dignity**. I'm very proud to be who I am."

DID YOU KNOW?

Scientists are interested in this rare condition. Danny has given blood for doctors to study. Other family members have too. In time, scientists may find the exact gene that causes this condition.

■ Answer the questions.

1. Circle *T* for true or *F* for false.

    A. Danny and his brother have starred in a TV show.   **T**   **F**

    B. The men in Danny's family have thicker hair than the women.   **T**   **F**

2. The parts of Danny's body with the least hair are his _____ .

3. In what way did Mundo Campo rescue Danny and his brother?

_____

_____

4. Having **dignity** means:

    A. having a good income

    B. having self-respect

    C. having many friends

5. Do you think that Danny's hair has anything to do with his acrobatic ability? Why or why not?

_____

_____

6. Do you think that most people would want to have hypertrichosis? Why or why not?

_____

_____

7. Do you think that Danny's early years were happy ones? Why or why not?

_____

_____

■ Choose one statement. Then, explain why you agree or disagree.

A. Being on a popular TV show would have earned Danny the love of many fans.

B. Scientists should leave Danny and his family alone.

A TANK OF A BIKE

■ Read the passage.
Heaviest Motorcycle, November 23, 2007

If you had an engine from a tank, what would you do with it? Tilo and Wilfried Niebel and their employees decided to build a motorcycle with theirs. In fact, they built the world's Heaviest Motorcycle.

The men used the engine from a T-55 Soviet tank. It had been built in Russia when it was still called the USSR, or Union of Soviet Socialist Republics. The motorcycle is in proportion to the engine. In other words, a really big engine makes a really big motorcycle! To make it easier to drive, they modeled the motorcycle after a World War II German motorbike with a **sidecar**. This sidecar has the hood and front end of a Soviet truck. If you look closely at the hood, you can see a **coat of arms** or crest. The crest has the letters *CCCP* on it. This means *USSR* in Russian.

The Niebels even used an anvil as a hood ornament on the sidecar! An anvil is a heavy iron block usually covered in a layer of steel. Anvils can weigh more than 200 pounds (90.7 kg).

So, if the hood ornament on the sidecar weighs 200 pounds (90.7 kg) or more, how much does the entire motorcycle weigh? The motorcycle weighs 5.24 tons (4.75 metric tons)! It took about 5,000 hours, or almost one year, to build. Tilo Niebel once said, "You don't get much more heavy metal than this." He was right about that!

■ Answer the questions.

1. What did the builders start with when they made the world's Heaviest Motorcycle?

_____

_____

2. What is a **coat of arms**?

    A. a winter coat

    B. a cape

    C. a crest

3. What is a **sidecar**?

_____

_____

4. Why do you think the sidecar makes it easier to drive the motorcycle?

_____

_____

5. Circle *T* for true or *F* for false.

    A. The Heaviest Motorcycle weighs 200 pounds (90.7 kg).   **T**   **F**

    B. The motorcycle took 5,000 days to build.   **T**   **F**

■ Choose one extension activity.

A. The Heaviest Motorcycle is built to be used on the road, but it is not licensed for road use. In other words, it is against the law to drive it on public roads. Can you imagine why? Make a list of reasons that the motorcycle would not be a practical vehicle for the road.

B. The crest of the former USSR is found on the sidecar of the motorcycle. Research to find out what a crest is and to learn if you have one for your family name. If you do not find one, draw your own after learning the meanings of some of the more popular symbols used on crests.

A GALAXY OF FUN

■ Read the passage.
Largest Amusement Park (Indoors)

Galaxyland is the largest indoor **amusement** park in the world! It is in Alberta, Canada. It can be found inside the West Edmonton Shopping Mall. The park covers 400,000 square feet (122 sq. km). That is the size of about 14 football fields put together!

Galaxyland was built for people to shop and have fun in. It has 27 rides, 30 skill games, and other attractions. It is so **enormous** that some people call it "the eighth wonder of the world."

Galaxyland is famous for having some of the largest indoor rides in the world. Its best-known ride is a roller coaster named Mindbender. This three-loop roller coaster is the longest and tallest in the world. It is 14 stories high and 4,198 feet (1,280 m) long. It is full of many twists and turns. The ride lasts a little over one minute! Now, that is a fast roller coaster!

Another favorite ride at Galaxyland is the Space Shot, which was once called the Drop of Doom. It is 13 stories high and is the tallest free fall ride in the world. The Space Shot is a quick drop to the bottom!

Everyone jump in the water! Galaxyland is also home to the largest indoor water park and wave pool! Young visitors especially enjoy the bumper boats there. With rides and games for everyone, Galaxyland is a popular place to visit and have fun!

Name_____ Date_____

■ Answer the questions.

1. Where is Galaxyland located?

_____

2. Galaxyland is the size of _____ football fields.

3. Galaxyland is so big it has been called _____ .

4. What is Galaxyland's most famous ride?

    A. bumper boats

    B. wave pool

    C. roller coaster

5. What does **amusement** mean? Why are some of the rides at Galaxyland so popular?

_____

_____

6. Which is an antonym for **enormous**?

    A. loud

    B. tiny

    C. large

■ Choose one extension activity.

A. Some indoor amusement parks are similar to Galaxyland. Find where they are located. What do they have in common with Galaxyland?

B. Discover who invented the roller coaster and where the first one was built. Then, create a design of your own roller coaster.

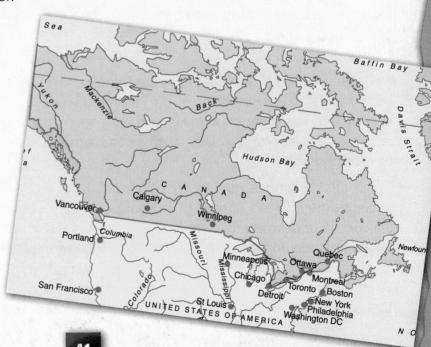

RUBBER BOY

■ Read the passage.
Most Flexible Man

Experts say that you should always stretch before you exercise. This keeps you from pulling a muscle. Many people do stretch. However, no one stretches quite like Daniel Browning Smith (USA). Smith calls himself Rubber Boy. He holds the Guinness World Records™ record for the Most Flexible Man in the world. Smith can bend backward really far. He goes back so far that the top of his head touches the seat of his pants. He also can twist his **torso** 180°.

Most **contortionists** are trained to bend in only one direction. But, Smith can bend in all directions. Imagine a tennis racket with all of the strings taken out. Smith can squeeze his whole body through the opening. He can do it in just 15 seconds. He also can cram his entire body into an 18-gallon (68-L) box. This box measures 13.5 × 16 × 19.5 inches (34.2 × 40.6 × 49.5 cm). That is about the size of a microwave oven.

Daniel Browning Smith is the most famous contortionist alive. He performs on TV dramas, talk shows, and late night shows. He also appears as an entertainer at sporting events, such as basketball and baseball games.

Contortion is not a new art form. It dates back to ancient times. Contortionists in ancient Greece, Egypt, and Rome performed for people. They also helped develop dance and art. Was there ever a contortionist as flexible as Daniel Browning Smith? We have no way of knowing for sure. Records were not kept in ancient times. Still, it seems doubtful that anyone could be more flexible than Rubber Boy.

DID YOU KNOW?
Daniel Browning Smith discovered his amazing ability when he was just four years old. He says that it happened while he was playing with his siblings (brothers and sisters). When Daniel jumped off his bed, he landed in a perfect split on the floor!

Name_____ Date_____

■ Answer the questions.

1. Circle *T* for true or *F* for false.

    A. Daniel Browning Smith can bend in all directions.   **T**   **F**

    B. Smith discovered his amazing talent when he was four years old. **T**   **F**

2. What unusual move can Smith do with a tennis racket?

_____

_____

3. What is the meaning of **torso**? Can you twist your torso?

_____

_____

4. Contortionists are people who:

    A. do card tricks to entertain people

    B. share knowledge with others

    C. can twist into unusual positions

5. Would you enjoy being a contortionist? Why or why not?

_____

_____

6. Do you think that Rubber Boy is a good name for Daniel Browning Smith? Why or why not?

_____

_____

■ Choose one statement. Then, explain why you agree or disagree.

A. Contortion is not like dance or art, so it should not be considered an art form.

B. Daniel Browning Smith should not use his unique physical ability to make money.

THIS MACHINE'S A MONSTER!

■ Read the passage.
Largest Land Vehicle, 1996

The largest machine that can move under its own power is the RB293 bucket-wheel **excavator**. The RB293 weighs a whopping 15,648 tons (14,196 metric tons)! It is hard to imagine how heavy that is. The weight of an average family car is about 2.5 tons (2.3 metric tons). So, the RB293 weighs more than 6,250 average cars. Now, that is hard to imagine!

The RB293's main job is digging and moving earth. It is used in **surface mining** for coal. Surface miners dig for coal or minerals near the surface of the ground instead of in deep underground caves and tunnels.

This monster machine is 722 feet (220 m) long and 310 feet (94.5 m) tall at its highest point. It can move almost 8.5 million cubic feet (240,700 cu. m) of dirt in one day. That means it can dig enough dirt to fill approximately 96 Olympic-sized swimming pools in just one day.

One thing that the RB293 cannot do is move quickly. It is not surprising that a machine this big is a slow mover. The RB293 moves about one-half mile (1 km) per hour. Only 14 miles (23 km) are between the place where the RB293 was built and the mine where it works. But, it took more than three weeks for the RB293 to crawl across the countryside to its new home.

■ **Answer the questions.**

1. What is **surface mining**?

_____

_____

2. Circle *T* for true or *F* for false.

   A. The RB293 has to be pulled by several large trucks.   T   F

   B. The RB293 is used to mine for gold.   T   F

3. What is an **excavator**?
   A. a large machine used to drill deep holes
   B. a heavy machine used to move earth
   C. a huge machine used to transport people

4. Why do you think the RB293 is so huge?

_____

_____

5. Does someone drive the RB293 to the digging site every day? Why or why not?

_____

_____

■ **Choose one extension activity.**

A. Many types of surface mining exist. Two types are strip mining and mountaintop removal. Research to learn how these are done. Then, write a paragraph about the advantages and disadvantages of surface mining.

B. When workers first moved the RB293 to the mine, they had to plan their trip carefully. Write a list of things that could make it difficult to move such a machine. What would get in the way? What would workers have to avoid?

IT'S A WRAP

■ Read the passage.
Largest Ball of Plastic Wrap, June 14, 2007

When Jake Lonsway (USA) was six years old, he decided that he wanted to try to break a world record. Lonsway and his parents searched for a record. They found the record for the Largest Ball of Plastic Wrap. They decided that was the one for Lonsway to break.

Lonsway's mother worked at a **plant** that had a lot of pieces of plastic wrap that could not be used. She began collecting them instead of throwing them away. Friends and neighbors also gave Lonsway rolls of plastic wrap.

Lonsway worked for eight months to create the giant ball in his garage. Sometimes, his parents helped him when he got tired. When Lonsway was seven years old, the ball was officially weighed and measured. It weighed 281.5 pounds (127.7 kg) and had a circumference of 11.5 feet (3.5 m). It set a new world record!

In 2009, Lonsway was still adding to the ball in his garage. The Mid-Michigan Children's Museum in Saginaw, Michigan, asked to put the ball on **exhibit**. Lonsway's parents thought that was a good idea because it took up a lot of space in the garage.

Name_____ Date_____

■ Answer the questions.

1. Jake Lonsway worked for _____ months to finish the ball. It officially

   weighed _____ pounds (_____ kg).

2. Another word for **exhibit** is:
   - **A.** experiment
   - **B.** habitat
   - **C.** display

3. Which is the definition of **plant** in the passage?
   - **A.** to put in the ground
   - **B.** a seedling or bush
   - **C.** a factory

4. Do you think Lonsway would have been able to break the world record if his mother had a different job? Why or why not?

   _____

   _____

5. Lonsway spent months working on his ball. List at least two things that could have made the project take so long.

   _____

   _____

■ Choose one extension activity.

A. Jake Lonsway and his parents have traveled with the ball to many places so that it could be put on exhibit during interviews. Write a paragraph or draw a diagram of how you would transport the ball to the different places.

B. Research to find the size and weight of the world's largest ball of aluminum foil and the world's largest ball of rubber bands. Make a chart that compares the sizes and weights of these two balls to Lonsway's ball of plastic wrap.

CROSSING THE OCEAN WITH NO FUEL

■ Read the passage.
Fastest Crossing of the Atlantic Ocean by Solar Power, February 2, 2007

A five-member crew crossed the Atlantic Ocean in just 29 days. And, their boat never used one drop of fuel! The *Sun21* became the fastest motorized **vessel** to cross the Atlantic Ocean using only solar power. The builders of the *Sun21* wanted to show that solar power is a perfect choice for boats and to raise awareness about cleaner energy.

Solar boats have electric engines. They are powered by special cells. These cells soak up sunlight and store it as energy. *Sun21* is able to store half of the energy that it **absorbs** in its batteries. So, it can run at night or on cloudy days using stored energy.

The crew set out from Switzerland in October 2006. They circled around the western edge of Europe. Then, they made a short stop in Spain. They left Spain for the Canary Islands in early January 2007. The Canary Islands were the last stop before heading to the open ocean. There, the crew purchased food and water for 40 days.

When they arrived in Martinique 29 days later, the crew had set a new world record. *Sun21* proved that solar energy can power boats. *Sun21*'s builders hope that their trip showed the world a better way to use energy and help the environment.

Name_____ Date_____

■ **Answer the questions.**

1. Why did the builders make *Sun21*?

_____

_____

2. Circle *T* for true or *F* for false.

A. *Sun21* uses solar power because it is cheaper than fuel.　　　　T　　　F

B. *Sun21* crossed the Atlantic Ocean in 29 days.　　　　T　　　F

3. What is a **vessel**?
    A. a ship
    B. a plane
    C. a bike

4. What does **absorbs** mean?
    A. soaks up
    B. pours
    C. loses

5. Circle *F* for fact or *O* for opinion.

A. All boats should use solar power.　　　　F　　　O

B. The *Sun21* can run on stored energy.　　　　F　　　O

C. The crew purchased more food and water than they needed.　　　F　　　O

■ **Choose one extension activity.**

A. Imagine that you are preparing for a long journey. Would you rather cross an ocean or a continent? Why? Make a list of the things you will need for your journey and how you will transport them.

B. The builders of *Sun21* built their boat for a good cause. Think of a cause that is important to you. Draw a poster, write a letter to the editor of your local newspaper, or write a commercial to call attention to your cause.

CHART-TOPPING TEEN

■ Read the passage.
Tallest Boy

Brenden Adams (USA) of Ellensburg, Washington, is so tall that every time he gets into his mom's SUV he has to sit in the third row. He folds down the middle row to make room for his long legs. Adams is the world's Tallest Boy under the age of 18. He topped the charts at 7 feet 4.6 inches (2.25 m) tall. He passed 7 feet when he was only 12 years old!

Can you imagine being so tall that you must duck to get through doorways? What if you wore shoes so large that you could not even special order them online? Adams has to deal with these things every day.

Adams says that he is just like other kids; he is just a little bit taller. His parents even had a special house built to make him more comfortable. In his new house, Adams does not bump his head everywhere he goes.

Adams' doctors were originally **stumped** about why he was growing so fast. He was a normal-sized baby, but he started growing quickly when he was four months old. By the time he was four years old, he was the size of a typical eight-year-old. And, when he was eight years old, Adams was the size of an average adult. Recently, his doctors think they have solved the mystery. They have given him medication to stop his growing. And, it seems to be working.

DID YOU KNOW?
The average adult male in the United States is 5 feet 9.2 inches (1.76 m) tall. The average adult female in the United States is 5 feet 3.8 inches (1.62 m) tall.

Adams has been a guest on many TV shows. One talk show host introduced Adams by satellite to an NBA basketball star. Like Adams, the NBA player is over 7 feet (2.13 m) tall. He can relate to Adams' struggles. The player invited Adams and his family to fly to Arizona where he lives. The NBA star even had his personal **tailor** make new clothes especially for Adams.

Name_____ Date_____

■ Answer the questions.

1. Circle *T* for true or *F* for false.

　　A. Brenden Adams must special order his shoes online.　　　**T**　　**F**

　　B. Adams' parents had a special house built for him.　　　**T**　　**F**

2. What does **stumped** mean?

　　A. easily explained

　　B. bored

　　C. totally confused

3. What does a **tailor** do?

　　A. makes clothes

　　B. builds cars

　　C. sells houses

4. Why would it be necessary for Adams to use a tailor?

_____

_____

5. How have doctors helped Adams?

_____

_____

■ Choose one extension activity.

A. Brenden Adams had the opportunity to meet a famous person whom he can relate to. Think of a famous person you can relate to. Why did you choose this person? Write about how you relate to this person and what you would do together if you met.

B. Choose four major foreign countries. Research the average heights in each country for males and females. Make a chart comparing your findings to the heights of males and females in your country.

SNAKE SNACK

■ Read the passage.
Most Worms Eaten in 30 Seconds, November 15, 2003

What is the strangest thing that you have ever eaten? Squid? Caviar? Frog legs? A man from India has eaten insects, lizards, and snakes. Manoharan Manu, or "Snake" Manu (India) as he likes to be called, began experimenting as an eight-year-old. He started performing strange tricks to amuse his classmates and get their attention.

At age 18, Manu found his specialty. He put a half-dead water snake into his nose and pulled it out of his mouth. This trick is what Manu calls "snake flossing." Since then, he has tried all kinds of live snakes. His favorites are small cobras because they are flexible. But, he has also used kraits, sand boas, and rat snakes. One time, a snake got stuck in his throat. Manu had to choose between biting the snake or being bitten by it. After that, he started eating the snakes that he inserted through his nose.

Manu's choice of **peculiar** snacks has made him a world record-holder. He holds the record for swallowing 200 live, slimy earthworms in 30 seconds. The thought of this may make you feel a little queasy. But, you may not know that earthworms can be a good source of **protein**. Protein is a nutrient needed for building strong muscles. However, protein also is found in a variety of more common foods, such as cheese, beans, or eggs.

Name_____ Date_____

■ Answer the questions.

1. What types of things has Manoharan Manu eaten?

    A. squid, insects, and snakes

    B. frog legs, caviar, and snakes

    C. lizards, insects, and snakes

2. What trick is Manu's specialty? Describe it.

    _____

    _____

3. What is the most likely reason Manu started performing these tricks?

    A. He likes the taste of the strange snacks.

    B. Manu likes the attention that he gets from performing such daring acts.

    C. He likes handling dangerous snakes.

4. Why does Manu prefer cobras to other snakes?

    _____

    _____

5. What event caused Manu to start eating snakes? What important choice did he have to make?

    _____

    _____

6. Manoharan Manu eats many **peculiar** snacks. How does this describe the snacks he eats?

    A. strange

    B. sweet

    C. difficult to find

7. What is a **protein**? How does protein help our bodies?

    _____

    _____

■ Choose one extension activity.

   A. Create a Venn diagram that compares and contrasts water snakes and cobras. Then, write a paragraph about each.

   B. Research the types of foods that provide protein for our bodies. Create a menu that features these food items.

REVIEW: ENGINEERING, SCIENCE & THE BODY

■ **Match the names with the correct clues.**

_____ **1.** Brenden Adams   **A.** circus acrobats

_____ **2.** Danny and Larry Gomez   **B.** motorcycle owners

_____ **3.** Daniel Browning Smith   **C.** contortionist

_____ **4.** Jake Lonsway   **D.** excavator

_____ **5.** Manoharan Manu   **E.** wrapper

_____ **6.** Mindbender   **F.** runs on solar power

_____ **7.** RB293   **G.** as tall as an NBA player

_____ **8.** *Sun21*   **H.** nicknamed "Snake"

_____ **9.** T-55 tank   **I.** Galaxyland's roller coaster

_____ **10.** Tilo and Wilfried Niebel   **J.** built in Russia

REVIEW: ENGINEERING, SCIENCE & THE BODY

■ **Circle the correct word to complete each sentence.**

1. The world's Heaviest Motorcycle has a (sidecar, roof).

2. Another word for a coat of arms is a (jacket, crest).

3. Galaxyland is the largest indoor (dog, amusement) park.

4. Daniel Browning Smith can twist his (neck, torso) 180°.

5. A heavy machine that moves earth is called an (irrigator, excavator).

6. A plant is another name for a (factory, hospital).

7. Special cells (absorb, reflect) sunlight to store solar power.

8. A vessel is a type of large (ship, truck).

9. A person who is puzzled or confused is (trunked, stumped).

10. Protein can be found in (food, machines).

THE ROOF OF THE WORLD

■ Read the passage.
Greatest Mountain Range on Earth

The Himalayan mountain range in Asia is the Greatest Mountain Range on Earth. Exactly 109 mountains in the world are over 24,000 feet (7,315 m). Ninety-six of them are in the Himalayas. You can see why the Himalayas are called "The Roof of the World."

The word *Himalaya* comes from an Indian language called Sanskrit. In that language, the word means "home of the snow." That is an **accurate** description. The peaks are so high and so cold that they always have snow on them.

DID YOU KNOW?
A lot of snow in the Himalayas melts each year. This mountain water is the source of three great world rivers. One is the Indus River in Pakistan. Another is the Yangtze River in China. The third is the Ganges River, which flows through India into Bangladesh.

Scientists think that they know how the Himalayas were formed. They say that Earth looked very different millions of years ago. At that time, India was connected to Africa. Then, movement deep inside Earth made the land shift. India broke away from Africa. Very slowly, it drifted to the northeast. About 50 million years ago, India hit Asia. It pushed against this continent with great force. The pressure slowly pushed up the land. That made huge mountains. India is still pushing against Asia. India moves about one-third of an inch (1 cm) about every six months. This means that the Himalayas are still being pushed up. The tallest mountains in the world are still growing!

Name_____ Date_____

■ Answer the questions.

1. Circle *T* for true or *F* for false.

    A. The Himalayan mountain range is new.   **T**   **F**

    B. Today, the Himalayas are part of Asia.   **T**   **F**

2. In Sanskrit the word *Himalaya* means _____

    _____

3. What does **accurate** mean? Give an example of a situation where it is important to be accurate.

    _____

    _____

4. According to this passage, in what ways does the world look different today than it did 100 million years ago?

    _____

    _____

5. The Himalayas are sometimes called "The Roof of the World." What would be another good nickname for them? Explain why you think this new nickname would fit.

    _____

    _____

■ Choose one extension activity.

    A. Write a poem describing how you think that it would feel to stand on the tallest mountain in the world.

    B. Design a travel brochure for a trip to the Himalayas.

THE NOT-SO-LIGHT BULB

■ Read the passage.
Heaviest Onion, 2005

It is easy to know when onions are being cut in the kitchen. Their strong odor makes most people cry. With more than 1,000 kinds to choose from, onions are a commonly grown vegetable in many gardens. Onions add flavor to a variety of **recipes**. They are used in salads, casseroles, and sauces. Onions are even on top of hamburgers. But, for some people, onions are a big business.

John Sifford (United Kingdom) is one person who knows a lot about growing onions. He holds the record for the Heaviest Onion. His giant onion was bigger than a human head! It weighed an amazing 16 pounds, 8 3/8 ounces (7.495 kg). That is the weight of a small dog! Mr. Sifford broke the former world record that had been held for 10 years. That onion weighed 15 pounds, 15 1/2 ounces (7.24 kg).

These onions and others like them are the stars at the **annual** Heaviest Onion Competition. This contest is held during the Harrogate Flower Show in the United Kingdom. Thousands of people from all over come to gaze at these amazing vegetables. Some people find their size a bit shocking.

Onions have been a part of our culture for centuries. Ancient Egyptians used onions as money. People in India used onions as medicine. In addition, onions are good for you. They are full of vitamins and minerals. Onions have been shown to fight heart disease and lower blood sugar. They help strengthen bones and protect against some cancers. With health benefits like these, maybe the tears are worth it.

WORLD-RECORD BREAKER!

16lb 8 $\frac{3}{8}$ oz

DID YOU KNOW?
Why do onions make us cry? Onions contain a certain chemical. It mixes with the moisture in your eyes. This produces a mild form of sulfuric acid. When that happens, the tears will flow. If you don't want to cry, here is a tip. Slice the onion from the top down. The chemical that causes tears is found at the base of the onion. If that doesn't work, you could always wear goggles!

■ Answer the questions.

1. With more than _____ kinds to choose from, onions are a

   common _____ grown in many gardens.

2. Why are onions offensive to some people?
   - **A.** They smell bad.
   - **B.** They make people laugh.
   - **C.** They taste bad.

3. Which definition best describes **recipes**?
   - **A.** types of medicine
   - **B.** kinds of food
   - **C.** instructions and ingredients for cooking

4. How did John Sifford achieve his world record? Where was this record achieved?

   _____

   _____

5. The Heaviest Onion Competition is an **annual** event. How often does this event happen?

   _____

   _____

6. Circle *T* for true or *F* for false.

   A. Some cultures have used onions as money.   **T**   **F**

   B. Some cultures have used onions as medicine.   **T**   **F**

■ Choose one extension activity.

A. Find out more about the ways onions are prepared
   and eaten. Create a booklet of onion recipes.

B. Onions are popular in many gardens. What
   type of care do they require? What type of
   soil do they need? Plan your own garden.
   What plants would you include?

A SURPRISE INSIDE

■ **Read the passage.**

Largest Amethyst Geode, October 27, 2008

Geodes are round or oval-shaped rocks that are plain on the outside. But, they are not your average rock. On the inside, some geodes are empty. Other geodes can have a beautiful surprise. When opened, they may have colorful minerals or crystals. Geodes can be a few inches (cm) or several feet (m) in size.

The Largest Amethyst Geode in the world was found in China. It is more than 9 feet (3 m) long and 7 feet (2.2 m) high. That makes it almost twice as big as a refrigerator. And, it weighs 13 tons (11.8 metric tons). That is as much as 65 refrigerators weigh!

Geodes are made when bubbles form in volcanic rock. As lava cools, bubbles become trapped. Those bubbles become geodes. Geodes take millions of years to form. When a geode is completely filled with crystals, it is called a **nodule**. Because geodes are rocks, they must be opened carefully. Some people use a chisel and a hammer. Others use a rock saw.

Geodes are found all over the world, but most are found in deserts, volcanic areas, or places with limestone. They have been found across the United States in places like California, Kentucky, and Iowa. Geodes can have many types of minerals. The most common are **quartz**, but other minerals can also be found. Amethysts are purple gemstones. Amethysts are a type of mineral often used in jewelry. Amethyst is also the traditional birthstone for February.

■ Answer the questions.

1. Circle *T* for true or *F* for false.

   A. All geodes have crystals inside.   T   F

   B. Geodes can be found all over the world.   T   F

2. As used in this passage, what is a **nodule**?

   _____

   _____

3. How are most geodes formed? How long does the process take?

   _____

   _____

4. What is an amethyst? What are amethysts commonly used for?

   _____

   _____

5. From this passage, you can conclude that **quartz** is a type of:
   A. geode
   B. amethyst
   C. mineral

■ Choose one extension activity.

A. Research places in the United States where geodes are found. Use a blank map of the United States to shade and label the types of minerals found there. Be sure to include a key to your map.

B. Make a scale drawing of the world's Largest Amethyst Geode. Include yourself in the picture. How tall are you compared to the geode?

FLOWER POWER

■ Read the passage.
Tallest Sunflower, August 17, 2009

Every summer, fields of tall, beautiful, yellow sunflowers stretch toward the sun. Sunflowers are native to North America. Many people use sunflowers as garden plants. Most sunflowers reach a height of 8 to 12 feet (2.4–3.7 m). Some sunflowers, however, really reach for the sky. A man named Hans-Peter Schiffer (Germany) grew the world's Tallest Sunflower. It was taller than a two-story building. His sunflower measured 26 feet 4 inches (8.03 m). That's quite a towering flower!

Mexican farmers first grew sunflowers more than 3,000 years ago. The early American Indians used them for food and hair oil. Sunflowers also have appeared in many famous paintings. Even the state of Kansas is nicknamed "The Sunflower State."

Sunflowers grow quickly, maturing from seeds to full grown plants in 120 days. The heads of the sunflower plant will turn to follow the sun. Because sunflowers are so tall, they must have strong roots. Their roots can be as deep as 9 feet (2.7 m). Sunflowers are ready to **harvest** in the autumn when they are dried and brown.

Today, the seeds of sunflowers are used for cooking oil and as snacks for birds and people. The seeds are a rich **source** of vitamins and minerals. The two kinds of sunflower seeds are black and striped. The black seeds are used for making oil. The striped seeds are used as food. It is no wonder that sunflowers are in gardens from Russia to Germany to Kansas!

DID YOU KNOW?

About 300 years ago, Russian leader Peter the Great saw sunflowers in Holland. He fell in love with them. He took some seeds back to his home in Russia. The sunflower became the national flower of Russia.

Name_____ Date_____

■ Answer the questions.

1. The first sunflowers were grown more than _____ years ago.

2. What did early American Indians use sunflowers for?

_____

_____

3. Which is the best definition of **harvest**?
   - **A.** to gather or collect
   - **B.** to sell for profit
   - **C.** to put together

4. How are the two types of sunflower seeds alike? Different?

_____

_____

5. Sunflower seeds are a rich **source** of vitamins and minerals. What are some other sources of vitamins and minerals?

_____

_____

6. Circle *F* for fact or *O* for opinion.

   A. Sunflowers become full grown plants in 120 days.   F   O

   B. Sunflowers are a delicious snack.   F   O

   C. Sunflowers improve the appearance of any garden.   F   O

■ Choose one extension activity.

A. Look at sunflower paintings by Vincent Van Gogh and Pablo Picasso. Create your own sunflower painting or sunflower seed art.

B. Research the different ways that sunflower seeds are used. How do sunflower seeds go from sunflower farms to our homes? Create a storyboard to explain the farm process. Be sure to describe sunflower seed products.

PICK THIS PECK OF PICKLES

■ Read the passage.

Most Cucumbers Harvested from One Plant in One Year, July 5, 2006

Do you know anyone who has grown cucumbers? If so, you know one thing. A single plant can give you a lot of cucumbers! Just how many cucumbers can one plant produce? The Guinness World Records™ record was set in the science section of a well-known Florida theme park. Workers began harvesting cucumbers from this plant on March 24, 2006. They ended on July 5, 2006. By then, the plant had yielded 2,563 cucumbers. These had a total weight of 2,078 pounds (943 kg). That is about as much as the total weight of 11 men. That is a lot of cucumber salad! Or, if you choose, that's a lot of pickles!

Cucumbers are a quick growing vegetable. That is one reason why gardeners like them so much. All you need is good, loose soil, lots of sun, and plenty of water. The cucumber plants will do the rest. You should give them quite a bit of space because these plants like to spread out. Cucumbers are ready for harvest in 50 to 70 days.

Cucumbers have been around for a long time. They **originated** in India over 3,000 years ago. Ancient poets sometimes wrote about them. Cucumbers are related to squash and cantaloupe. They are all members of the **gourd** family. Cucumbers have a light, pleasant taste. That makes them popular around the world. Right now, someone somewhere is slicing a freshly picked cucumber and taking the first bite.

■ Answer the questions.

1. Cucumbers are ready to be harvested after growing for _____ .
   A. 7 to 10 days
   B. 15 to 30 days
   C. 50 to 70 days
   D. 70 to 100 days

2. What do you need to grow cucumbers?

   _____

   _____

3. Something that **originated** is something that:
   A. started
   B. was copied
   C. was rejected

4. Based on the information in the passage, do you think that members of the **gourd** family are safe to eat? Why or why not?

   _____

   _____

5. Why do you think that ancient poets wrote about cucumbers?

   _____

   _____

■ Choose one extension activity.

A. Create your own poem about cucumbers. See if you can write a poem that rhymes.
B. Take a survey of your friends. Ask if they prefer cucumbers plain or made into pickles. How many of them do not like cucumbers at all? Share your findings with your friends.

CLIMBING AN IRON ROAD

■ Read the passage.

Highest Iron Road (Via Ferrata), February 25, 2009

Via ferrata is an Italian term. It means "iron road." In 2009, the world's Highest Via Ferrata was finished. It is on Mount Kinabalu in Borneo. Borneo is an island in Asia. It is part of the country of Malaysia. The via ferrata begins at 11,190 feet 11 inches (3,411 m). It goes up to 12,388 feet 5 inches (3775.8 meters).

This iron road is not a road in the usual sense of the word. It is a set of rungs, rails, and cables. These are **embedded** into the mountain's rock face. They were put there so that all people could enjoy the beauty of the mountain. Before the iron road was built, Kinabalu was **accessible** only to strong rock climbers. Now, all that has changed. If you can climb a ladder, you can climb Kinabalu. It has been climbed by people as young as 10 and as old as 70. Of course, you should be in good health. Just taking a breath is a little harder when you are up this high because less oxygen is in the air. Also, you should not be afraid of heights. That could be a real problem when you are hanging from a ladder at 12,000 feet (3,657.6 m)!

The oldest iron road is in the mountains of Europe. It was built more than 150 years ago. Later, more of these paths were built. Soldiers built some during World War I to get supplies over steep mountains. Today, more than 300 iron roads are in the world. Most are in Europe, but a few are in North America and New Zealand. The highest, however, is on the island of Borneo.

Name_____ Date_____

■ **Answer the questions.**

1. Circle *T* for true or *F* for false.

    A. The first via ferrata was built in New Zealand.   T   F

    B. Via ferrata means "ladder road."   T   F

2. Mount Kinabalu is located on the island of _____ .

3. Something that is **embedded** is:
    A. within something else
    B. lying on top
    C. not intended to be permanent

4. When the suffix *-ible* is added to a word, it means "able to." What does **accessible** mean? Give an example of another word that contains the suffix *-ible*. What does it mean?

    _____

    _____

5. Why do you think that children under 10 years old have not climbed this iron road?

    _____

    _____

6. Do you think that "iron road" is a good name for this path? Why or why not? If you had to pick a new name for it, what would you choose and why?

    _____

    _____

7. Do you think that you would enjoy climbing the world's highest iron road? Why or why not?

    _____

    _____

■ **Choose one extension activity.**

    A. Investigate Borneo. List five facts you learn about this island.

    B. Research the world's oldest via ferrata. Where in Europe is it? Who built it? Is it still being used?

Experience the **world's highest** and **asia's first VIA FERRATA** on MT KINABALU

QUICK, BEFORE IT MELTS!

■ Read the passage.

Largest Ice Village, December 2002

Most houses are built to last a long time. That is not true of igloos. These huts are typically constructed of ice. They last only a few months in the winter. They melt away in the warm spring sun. Still, that does not stop people from building them. In 2002, the Largest Ice Village ever made was built in the town of Jukkasjärvi, Sweden. This town is 120 miles (193 km) north of the Arctic Circle. The ice village that was built there had 140 igloos. It was made to provide **lodging** for 700 guests coming to town to attend a conference.

The conference itself was held at the famous IceHotel. This is a real hotel made entirely of ice. The IceHotel has guest rooms, a chapel, and even a movie theater. The first IceHotel was built in 1992. It became an instant hit.

The hotel has to be rebuilt every year, of course. The construction starts in mid-November. Ice blocks are harvested from the Tome River. Then, they are put in place. The IceHotel stays open until spring. Then, it melts away. People aren't too sad, though. They know a new IceHotel will be built in a few months.

DID YOU KNOW?

Why would anyone want to go to a dark, cold place like Jukkasjärvi, Sweden, in the middle of winter? One reason is to stay at the IceHotel. Another reason is to see the "northern lights." These are bright, colorful flashes of light that appear in the night sky. They are most common near arctic areas.

■ Answer the questions.

1. The town of Jukkasjärvi, Sweden, is 120 miles (193 km) _____ of the Arctic Circle.

2. Circle *T* for true or *F* for false.

   A. Most igloos are built to last between five and ten years.   **T**   **F**

   B. The IceHotel must be rebuilt every year.   **T**   **F**

3. Igloos melt when
   A. nearby rivers dry up.
   B. the weather gets warm.
   C. salt from the atmosphere coats the ice.

4. What does **lodging** mean as it is used in this passage?

   _____

   _____

5. List three items you would want to pack if you were staying at the IceHotel. List three items you would not pack.

   _____

   _____

6. Would you like to stay at the IceHotel? Why or why not?

   _____

   _____

■ Choose one extension activity.

A. Draw a picture showing what you imagine a guest room inside the IceHotel looks like. Be sure to include details in your drawing.
B. Write a poem describing how you think it would feel to live in an ice village.

SAND MAGIC

■ Read the passage.

Most Sand Castles Built in One Hour, June 14, 2007

How many sand castles do you think you could build in an hour? You would have to build a lot to beat the Guinness World Records™ record. It was set by a team of employees in France. They built 520 sand castles in just one hour. It must have been a really sandy beach!

For many beachgoers, building sand castles is a simple **pastime**. For others, it is much more than that. It is an art form. Some people even have turned it into a competition. Believe it or not, a World Championship of Sand Sculpting exists. Some very accomplished artists compete in it. No ordinary sand castle will win this event. It takes a clever design to do well. Just how **intricate** are the creations? In the past, sand artists have sculpted mermaids. One group of Russian artists created a series of sculptures that showed events from Russian history.

People who want to be in the world championship first must win smaller contests. One of these is held at Hampton Beach in New Hampshire. Artists are assigned spots on the beach. They also each get 10 tons (9.07 metric tons) of fresh sand. After that, it is up to the artist's imagination.

DID YOU KNOW?

Judging the best sand sculptures is not easy. Judges rate each one in several categories. These include skill and degree of difficulty. They also rate the "Wow" factor. One judge explained, "The judging takes three or four hours of intense debate."

■ Answer the questions.

1. The record number of sand castles built in one hour is _____ .

2. What does **pastime** mean? Name three pastimes you enjoy.

   _____

   _____

3. Something that is **intricate** is:
   A. containing many different and connected parts
   B. able to fit inside something larger
   C. considered beautiful by everyone

4. If you were given 10 tons of sand and asked to make a sand sculpture, what would you try to make? Explain why this would be your choice.

   _____

   _____

5. Would you rather participate in a team competition for the Most Sand Castles Built in One Hour or in an individual competition for the best sand sculpture? Why?

   _____

   _____

6. Imagine that you have just won the World Championship of Sand Sculpting. How do you think that you would feel when wind and water begin to eat away at your creation?

   _____

   _____

■ Choose one extension activity.

A. Use sugar cubes and water to design a small sculpture of your own. Be sure to give the finished product a title.

B. Write a short radio commercial advertising the World Championship of Sand Sculpting. The commercial should encourage people to enter or to watch this competition.

WHAT'S A CHINESE LIZARD-WING?

■ Read the passage.
Largest Sinosauropteryx Fossil, January 2, 2009

In 2009, the world's Largest Sinosauropteryx **Fossil** was discovered. It was found in China. It is 12 feet 5 inches (3.8 m) long. That is about as long as a car. It is now housed in a museum in China's Shandong Province.

A Sinosauropteryx is a kind of dinosaur. Its name means "Chinese lizard-wing." Scientists think that it is an ancestor of today's birds. This is the oldest dinosaur with feathers ever found. It lived over 120 million years ago.

The feathers of this dinosaur were 1.5 inches (3.8 cm) long. That makes them about as long as sewing needles. Even though this animal had feathers, it was not a flying dinosaur. Instead, it walked on two long legs. The creature's soft feathers were just for **insulation**. They helped keep the dinosaur warm. They formed a kind of mane along the dinosaur's back.

Scientists have found several fossils of this type of dinosaur. Some show what was in the creatures' stomachs when they died. Some show unlaid eggs. Scientists have learned a great deal from these things. They know that this dinosaur ate meat. To hunt, it used its two short arms. It also used its many sharp teeth. Its diet was mostly small animals and insects. Some people think that this dinosaur is particularly interesting because of its feathers. These feathers suggest that birds really did come from dinosaurs.

■ Answer the questions.

1. The feathers of the Sinosauropteryx were about as long as

    A. pencils.

    B. sewing needles.

    C. broom handles.

2. Circle *T* for true or *F* for false.

    A. A Sinosauropteryx had two legs.   **T**   **F**

    B. Some fossils show what was in animals' stomachs.   **T**   **F**

3. A **fossil** is:

    A. a nest used by a creature that lived long ago

    B. a picture that scientists create to show what a dinosaur looked like

    C. the hardened remains of some plant or animal

4. What does **insulation** mean in this passage? Describe a situation where insulation would be helpful.

_____

_____

5. How do you think that the ability to fly might help a creature hunt? How do you think that it might make hunting more difficult?

_____

_____

6. Do you think that the Sinosauropteryx would be as interesting to scientists if this creature lived only a few million years ago? Why or why not?

_____

_____

■ Choose one statement. Then, explain why you agree or disagree.

    A. Fossils should be left where they are found instead of being moved into museums.

    B. People spend too much time studying the past and not enough time thinking about the future.

A SALUTE TO THE GENERAL

GENERAL SHERMAN

■ Read the passage.
Largest Living Tree, 2002

The world's Largest Living Tree is General Sherman. It is a giant sequoia growing in the Sequoia National Park in California. When General Sherman was measured in 2002, it stood 271 feet (82.6 m) tall. It is **estimated** to weigh four million pounds (1,814 metric tons)! It would take at least 267 adult male African elephants to equal the weight of this tree! General Sherman is also estimated to contain enough wood to make over five billion matchsticks. The tree is as wide as a three-lane highway.

General Sherman is thought to be 2,100 years old. An average giant sequoia can grow as tall as a 26-story building. Sequoias grow so large because they grow quickly and live for a long time.

Sequoias are strong trees. But, they have shallow roots. The hard ground makes it even harder for their roots to dig in deeply. Once the trees grow tall enough, they are at risk for toppling over if their roots are not secure.

Millions of years ago, sequoias grew all over North America. Then, the weather turned colder and drier. These trees need warm weather to live. Now, when people visit the remaining sequoia forests, they walk and drive all over the ground. This makes the ground hard. It is difficult for a sequoia's roots to soak water from hard ground. These are all reasons that the number of sequoias continues to shrink.

Name_____ Date_____

■ Answer the questions.

1. General Sherman was _____ tall when it was measured in 2002. It is estimated to weigh _____ pounds!

2. How many male African elephants equal the weight of General Sherman?
   A. 26.7
   B. 267
   C. 2,670

3. What does **estimated** mean?
   A. measured exactly
   B. roughly calculated
   C. hoped

4. List two things in nature that are threatening the survival of giant sequoias.

   _____

   _____

5. What can people do to protect the giant sequoias?

   _____

   _____

■ Choose one extension activity.

A. Giant sequoias are struggling to survive in North America. Research to find out how people can help. Make a flier showing people how they can help save the sequoias.

B. Imagine that you are living in a tree house at the top of General Sherman. Write a story or poem about what life is like and what you can see from your home.

REVIEW: EARTH EXTREMES

■ **Complete the passage by writing the correct word in each blank.**

Let's track some earthly record-breakers in a trip around the world! We'll start in Asia,

with the greatest mountain range in the world, the _____ mountains. If you
(1)

like that view, you'll love a climb along Borneo's via ferrata, the highest _____
(2)

_____ on Earth.
(3)

We continue through Asia to visit a Chinese museum. It won't be hard for us to spot the

Chinese lizard-wing, a dinosaur _____ the size of a car. And we won't need
(4)

glasses to find the Largest Amethyst _____ in the world. It's twice the size of
(5)

a refrigerator, and it's also in China.

California has geodes, too, but let's look at a gem of a different kind. We'll travel east to

North America and to _____ National Park. Things will really be looking up
(6)

there, when we gaze at General Sherman, the Largest Living Tree.

Let's head south of California. Farmers in _____ first planted sunflower
(7)

seeds more than 3,000 years ago. They'd be shocked to see the two-story-tall sunflower

grown by Hans-Peter Schiffer of Germany. A quick stop in Florida and we'll enjoy a crunchy

snack when we pick a few of the 2,563 _____ growing on just one plant!
(8)

We're bound to find a beach in Florida, but it will be more fun to play in the sand in France.

Let's go to Europe, where a French team holds the world record of 520 _____
(9)

_____ built in one hour!
(10)

Too hot for you? Then, we'll head north to Sweden. We can spend a few days chilling in

an _____ village. Better still, how about checking into a room at the famous
(11)

_____? Now, that's really cool!
(12)

Our final stop is the United Kingdom, to attend the annual Heaviest _____
(13)

Competition! The record-breaker weighed more than 16.5 pounds (7.5 kg).

REVIEW: EARTH EXTREMES

■ **Fill in the missing letter for each vocabulary word to discover the secret message. Then, write the secret message.**

N O D U L _____

Q U _____ R T Z

_____ E C I P E S

I N T R I C A _____ E

_____ A R V E S T

F O S S _____ L

_____ O U R C E

_____ S T I M A T E D

E _____ H I B I T

P A S _____ I M E

A C C U _____ A T E

O R I G I N A T _____ D

E _____ B E D D E D

A C C E S S I B L _____

Secret message: _____ _____ _____ _____ _____   _____ _____

_____ _____ _____ _____ _____ _____ _____ !

YOU'LL FLIP OVER THIS

■ Read the passage.
Earliest Landed Wheelchair Backflip, October 25, 2008

Whoosh! Here comes Aaron Fotheringham (USA)! Aaron is skateboarding in his wheelchair! He rolls down a ramp and jumps a curb. He even can flip in the air! That is how he landed his first wheelchair backflip. Aaron performed this trick in Doc Romeo Park in Las Vegas, Nevada.

Aaron is a special kind of **athlete**. He cannot walk, but that has never slowed him down. His interest in skateboarding began when he was a young boy. He watched his older brother skate at a nearby park. His brother thought that Aaron should skateboard in his wheelchair. Aaron practiced hard to learn to use his wheelchair. At age eight, he was able to perform tricks with it. Aaron was 14 years old when he set the Guinness World Records™ record for the Earliest Landed Wheelchair Backflip.

Aaron wins many awards and contests. His nickname is Wheels. People like to watch him in competition. He is famous for his spins and jumps and for wearing a seat belt, helmet, and pads. Yet Aaron's greatest pride is working with children just like him. He shows them what they can do in a wheelchair. Aaron is a hero to both children and adults.

Name_____ Date_____

■ Answer the questions.

1. What made Aaron Fotheringham want to learn skateboarding?

_____

_____

2. Aaron is able to use his wheelchair like a skateboard because
   - **A.** he uses his hands to balance.
   - **B.** he practices a lot.
   - **C.** he moves to one side of his wheelchair.

3. What is Aaron's greatest pride?
   - **A.** his work with children
   - **B.** his world record
   - **C.** his spins and jumps

4. Circle *T* for true or *F* for false.

   A. Aaron was eight years old when he set his world record.   **T**   **F**

   B. Aaron performed his backflip in Los Angeles, California.   **T**   **F**

5. What is an **athlete**? Why is Aaron a special kind of athlete?

_____

_____

6. Why might it be more difficult for Aaron to be in a skateboarding competition?

_____

_____

■ Choose one extension activity.

A. Find information on competitions involving athletes with disabilities.

B. Aaron is proud of what he can do with his wheelchair. Write about something that makes you feel proud of yourself.

79

WHERE DOES THIS PIECE GO?

■ Read the passage.
Largest Jigsaw Puzzle, November 3, 2002

Many people like doing jigsaw puzzles. No jigsaw puzzle, however, is bigger than the one put together in Hong Kong. This puzzle had 21,600 pieces. It took 777 people to complete it. The puzzle was 58,435.1 square feet (5,428.8 sq. m). That is about the size of a football field!

The very first jigsaw puzzle may have been made by John Spilsbury. He lived in the 1700s. Spilsbury was a mapmaker. He took a map of Europe, and he cut it up to form puzzle pieces. Each country was one piece. One hundred years later, people began to cut puzzle pieces with a special saw. These were the first true jigsaw puzzles.

During the Great Depression of the 1930s, jigsaw puzzles became popular. Many people had no jobs. They had very little money. They welcomed the chance to have fun.

People today still like jigsaw puzzles. Doing a puzzle can help **relieve** stress. It is a nice way to spend time with friends. Also, it helps keep your mind sharp. Even if your next puzzle does not have 21,600 pieces, it can still be a fun challenge!

DID YOU KNOW?
Today, most puzzles are made in factories. In earlier times, however, people cut pieces by hand. They traced a design on the back of a piece of wood. They followed these lines when cutting out the pieces. You can still see the pencil marks on the back of very old puzzle pieces.

■ Answer the questions.

1. John Spilsbury made the first puzzle by cutting up a

   A. map.

   B. photo.

   C. magazine.

2. Circle *T* for true or *F* for false.

   A. Most puzzles today are made in factories.   **T**   **F**

   B. People used a special drill to cut puzzle pieces.   **T**   **F**

3. What does **relieve** mean? What are other good ways to relieve stress?

   _____

   _____

4. Putting together the world's Largest Jigsaw Puzzle required

   A. teamwork.

   B. luck.

   C. knowledge.

5. Puzzles are a low-cost form of entertainment. What other forms of entertainment can you name that do not cost much money?

   _____

   _____

6. Would you rather do a jigsaw puzzle by yourself or be one of 777 people to put together the world's Largest Jigsaw Puzzle? Explain your answer.

   _____

   _____

■ Choose one extension activity.

A. Make your own 20-piece puzzle. Use thin cardboard for the backing. Draw a simple design on the front, then cut out the pieces. See how long it takes your friends to put your puzzle together.

B. Do you enjoy crossword puzzles, word scrambles, mazes, or word search puzzles? Research the history of your favorite kind of puzzle.

AN EGG, A SPOON, AND A MAN WHO SETS RECORDS

■ Read the passage.
Fastest Mile Carrying an Egg on a Spoon in the Mouth, April 27, 2007

Ashrita Furman (USA) loves to break world records. One record that he broke involved a spoon, an egg, but no eating. Furman became the fastest person to run a mile (1.6 km) while carrying an egg on a spoon held in his mouth. His time was just 9 minutes, 29 seconds. That is quite a **feat**.

That is just one of Furman's records. He holds many others. He has eaten the most candy-covered chocolates in one minute using chopsticks. He has sliced the most apples in midair in one minute using a Japanese sword. In fact, he holds the Guinness World Records™ record for setting the most records! He has set more than 250 records. Many have been broken later by others. But, Furman still holds more records than anyone else.

Furman will go almost anywhere for a record. He has set at least one record on every continent. Thinking of Australia? Furman Hula-hooped® the fastest mile there. What about Antarctica? Furman covered the fastest mile on a pogo stick there. Furman also likes to break records near or on famous places. Bouncing on a hoppity hop, or kangaroo ball, along the Great Wall of China is an example. He set the record for the fastest mile bouncing on a kangaroo ball at this wall!

In his free time, Furman likes to **meditate**. He says it helps him in many ways. He says, "If one can be in touch with one's inner spirit, anything is possible."

■ Answer the questions.

1. Circle *T* for true or *F* for false.

    A. Ashrita Furman has set more world records than anyone else.   **T**   **F**

    B. Furman broke a pogo stick record in Antarctica.   **T**   **F**

2. What did Furman do at the Great Wall of China?

_____

_____

3. What is the definition of **feat**? What is one feat that you have witnessed?

_____

_____

4. To **meditate** means to:
    A. sing a song loudly
    B. exercise for an extended period of time
    C. think or focus deeply

5. Do you think that Furman sounds like a timid, fearful man? Why or why not?

_____

_____

■ Choose one extension activity.

A. Furman has set records on every continent. Pick one continent and gather information about it. Write a list of five facts that you discover.

B. It took Furman 9 minutes, 29 seconds to run a mile while carrying an egg on a spoon held in his mouth. What is the record for fastest mile run without carrying anything? Find out who set this record. Then, research to learn more about this person. Write a paragraph about what you learned.

SPEEDY PICKUP

■ Read the passage.

Fastest Production Pickup Truck, May 25, 2006

This pickup truck can really move! It holds the record for the Fastest Production Pickup Truck. A truck is called a **production truck** when a company has made a large number of them to sell. It is a standard truck. The company that makes this pickup truck has been selling them for 15 years.

To help set the record, the truck company had a professional driver on its side. Race car driver Mark Skaife (Australia) drove the truck. He was able to achieve a speed of 168.7 miles (271.4 km) per hour. The record was set in a **prohibited** area in Australia.

Skaife is a famous race car driver. Many people in Australia say that he is the best. He has had a long career. He started racing go-karts when he was 17 years old. A few years later, he began racing cars. Throughout his 22-year career, Skaife won many races.

Although Skaife no longer races, he certainly stays busy. Skaife works in TV and radio. He also helps design tracks. He focuses on safety. Skaife has designed many racetracks around Australia.

Name_____ Date_____

■ Answer the questions.

1. Who is Mark Skaife?

_____

_____

2. What does the term **production truck** mean?

_____

_____

3. How fast did the fastest production pickup truck go?

_____

_____

4. Circle *F* for fact or *O* for opinion.

    A. Mark Skaife is the best race car driver ever.   **F**   **O**

    B. Go-karts are more fun to drive than cars.   **F**   **O**

    C. Mark Skaife raced for 22 years.   **F**   **O**

5. An area that is **prohibited** could also be described as being:

    A. off-limits   **B.** a place open to the public

    C. a restaurant   **D.** free

6. Do you think that information is missing from the passage? What other facts would you like to know about this record?

_____

_____

■ Choose one extension activity.

A. The world's fastest production truck is from Australia. Locate Australia on a map and research the country. Is this a place where you would like to live? Why or why not?

B. Mark Skaife designs racetracks. Draw a sketch of your own racetrack. What factors will you consider when designing your track?

A SNEAKER FOR A GIANT

■ Read the passage.
Largest Sports Shoe/Sneaker, March 26, 2009

Can you imagine a sneaker that is larger than a car? Such a sneaker was actually built. A large company in the United Kingdom had it made. The company wanted to support the United Kingdom's Race for Life. This event raises money for cancer research. To **promote** the race, the company ordered the largest sneaker in the world. It measured 13 feet 1 inch (4 m) long. It was 5 feet 2 inches (1.6 m) wide. Its height was 5 feet 6 inches (1.7 m). This shoe is bigger than most cars.

How tall would a person have to be to wear this sneaker? This person would need to be an 87-foot-tall (27-m-tall) giant! He would be about as tall as a nine-story building! His legs would be very long. Each step he took would cover about 36 feet (11 m). The Race for Life is three miles (5 km). The average female runner takes 7,246 strides to cover the course. Our imagined giant would need just 454 strides to travel the same distance.

This giant sneaker was built to the standards of a regular sneaker. It was made with **authentic** materials, such as leather and rubber. It took three months (more than 800 hours of labor) to finish. Of course, no shoe is complete without a shoelace. The lace for this shoe was 59 feet (18 m) long. On a Little League baseball field, the lace could stretch almost all of the way from home plate to first base!

Name_____ Date_____

■ Answer the questions.

1. Circle *T* for true or *F* for false.

    A. A United Kingdom company had this shoe made
       to sell in stores.   **T**   **F**

    B. It took three months to finish making this shoe.   **T**   **F**

2. How tall would a person probably need to be to wear this sneaker?

_____

_____

3. In this passage, **authentic** means:

    A. real

    B. expensive

    C. used

4. What does **promote** mean in this passage? What is one group or cause you would like to help promote?

_____

_____

5. The sneaker has the same colors as the British flag. Do you think that this is important in any way? Explain your answer.

_____

_____

6. Do you think that building this giant sneaker was a good way to support Race for Life? Why or why not?

_____

_____

■ Choose one extension activity.

A. Imagine that you have been given this sneaker. Write a paragraph describing what you plan to do with it. What uses could you find for it? Explain.

B. Race for Life raises money for cancer. Imagine that you have been asked to raise money for a charity. Organize an outline of the event you would hold. Include who, what, when, where, and why.

HAND-TO-HAND GAMES

■ Read the passage.
Largest Tournament of Rock, Paper, Scissors, April 11, 2008

The students at Brigham Young University in Utah wanted to raise money for charity. So, they put together the largest rock, paper, scissors tournament ever held. A total of 793 people participated.

During the tournament, the number of players was slowly whittled down. This was done by a series of **eliminations**. In time, Kenny Matthews won.

> **DID YOU KNOW?**
> An official World Rock Paper Scissors Society exists. It offers advice for beginning players. For instance, it suggests that you think twice before using rock, paper, scissors to make an important decision.

Here is a quick lesson on how to play. Face your opponent. Close one hand into a fist. Now flex and straighten that arm three times. The third time you straighten your arm, shape your fist into your throw of choice. It may be a rock (fist), paper (flat hand), or scissors (two fingers split apart). Your opponent also picks a "throw." Both of you must reveal your throws at the same moment.

Rock beats (or blunts) scissors. Scissors beat (or cut) paper. Paper beats (or covers) rock. People often play "best two out of three." That means that the first player to win two times is the **victor**. No matter how many times you play it, rock, paper, scissors remains a tricky, fun game.

■ Answer the questions.

1. When people play games of rock, paper, scissors, they often play the best two out of
   - **A.** three.
   - **B.** five.
   - **C.** ten.

2. In this game, you make scissors
   - **A.** by straightening out your elbow.
   - **B.** with two fingers split apart.
   - **C.** by slapping your hands together.

3. What does **eliminations** mean in this passage?

   _____

   _____

4. What is a **victor**? Name a time when you have been a victor.

   _____

   _____

5. Do you think that it is important for both players to reveal their throws at the same time? Why or why not?

   _____

   _____

■ Choose one extension activity.

A. Working in a group, hold your own mini-tournament of rock, paper, scissors. Try to predict what the winning throw will be in the final round. Compare your predictions with your groups' guesses.

B. The World Rock Paper Scissors Society advises that you should "think twice" before using rock, paper, scissors to make an important decision. Explain why you agree or disagree.

FANCY FOOTWORK

■ Read the passage.
Most Soccer Ball Touches in 30 Seconds (Female), February 23, 2008

Chloe Hegland (Canada) has fancy feet. She holds the Guinness World Records™ record for Most Soccer Ball Touches in 30 Seconds by a Female. Touching the soccer ball is also known as **juggling**. Juggling in soccer is keeping the ball in the air by bouncing it off different body parts. Players are supposed to use only their feet, legs, and heads. Hegland juggled for 30 seconds and touched the ball 163 times.

Hegland is 10 years old and lives in Canada. She broke the record in Spain in front of her father and two other witnesses. She also has beaten the male record. The male record is 147.

Hegland also broke the record for most touches in 60 seconds. She juggled the ball 339 times! She said that breaking the record was fun and easier than she thought it would be. Amazingly enough, Hegland has been playing soccer for only two years. Watch for Hegland on the soccer field. It sounds like she is already a **master**.

DID YOU KNOW?
The world record for juggling a ball non-stop is 19 hours and 30 minutes. Martinho Eduardo Orige from Brazil has the fancy feet that set the record.

Name_____ Date_____

■ **Answer the questions.**

1. What does **juggling** a soccer ball involve?

_____

_____

2. By how many touches does Chloe Hegland's record beat the male record?

_____

3. A person who is a **master** of a skill:

    A. doesn't know how to do it

    B. is learning how to do it

    C. knows how to do it well

4. Circle *T* for true or *F* for false.

    A. Hegland lives in Canada.   **T**   **F**

    B. Next, Hegland wants to break the record for most touches in 60 seconds. **T**   **F**

5. How do you think that juggling the ball might help a player during a soccer game? Is this a good skill for a player to have?

_____

_____

6. What do you think is the most interesting fact about Hegland?

_____

7. The passage reads, "Amazingly enough, Hegland has been playing soccer for only two years." Why is it amazing that Hegland has been playing soccer for only two years?

_____

_____

■ **Choose one extension activity.**

    A. What questions would you like to ask Chloe Hegland? Write a letter to her.

    B. Ask a friend to time you while you try to juggle a ball for 30 seconds. Can you keep the ball in the air for 30 seconds? How many "touches" can you get?

© **Carson-Dellosa**   **91**

A VERY LONG RIDE

■ Read the passage.
Longest Bicycle, December 11, 2002

This bicycle was not made for quick trips to the market. Finding a place to park it would definitely be a challenge. You would need several parking spaces! The Longest Bicycle in the world is 92 feet (28 m) long. It is considered the longest *true* bicycle. That is because, like a **typical** bicycle, it has two wheels. It does not have an extra wheel to help steady it.

A group of **engineering** students at Delft University of Technology built the bike. The school is in the Netherlands. Engineering is the science of designing and building things. Engineering students plan and create in a special way. This bicycle is a good example of what they can think up.

The longest bicycle was taken out for a spin in the Netherlands. The bike went more than 328 feet (100 m).

DID YOU KNOW?
Bicycles are one of the best ways to travel. It takes less energy to pedal a bike than to walk. About one billion bicycles are in the world. Almost 400 million of them are in China.

Name_____ Date_____

■ Answer the questions.

1. Who built the world's Longest Bicycle?

_____

2. What does it mean to say the Longest Bicycle is a "true bicycle"?

_____

_____

3. An antonym for **typical** is:

   A. average

   B. normal

   C. special

4. Circle *F* for fact or *O* for opinion.

   A. The best engineering students are from the Netherlands.   **F**   **O**

   B. It takes less energy to pedal a bike than it does to walk.   **F**   **O**

   C. The longest bicycle is really cool.   **F**   **O**

5. What does an **engineering** student study?

_____

_____

6. If you were an engineering student, what would you want to work on?

_____

_____

■ Choose one extension activity.

A. Research bicycles. What did the first bicycle look like? How is it similar to and different from bicycles today?

B. Write a song about riding the world's Longest Bicycle and trying to find a parking space.

WHEELCHAIR WHEELIE

■ Read the passage.
Longest Wheelie in a Wheelchair, August 8, 2009

Michael Miller (USA) does not like to keep four wheels on the ground. He would rather travel on two! Miller holds the Guinness World Records™ record for the Longest Wheelie in a Wheelchair. Miller rode 10 miles (16 km) on the back wheels of his wheelchair in 2009. It took him 3 hours, 55 minutes.

DID YOU KNOW?
Spina bifida is the most common permanently disabling birth defect in the United States. No known cure exists.

Miller is 19 years old and from Wisconsin. He was born with a birth defect called spina bifida. Because of this disease, he cannot walk. But, not being able to walk does not keep Miller down.

Miller popped his first wheelie when he was four. He has wanted to break a world record for a long time. Many surgeries kept him from doing it. But, he held on to his dream. He joined the YMCA and worked very hard. He spent many hours training. He was **dedicated**.

Miller wanted to send a message to the world. He thinks that people **underestimate** those who have disabilities. He wanted to prove that people with disabilities can do great things.

Name_____ Date_____

■ Answer the questions.

1. What world record does Michael Miller hold?

_____

_____

2. How do you do a wheelie?

_____

_____

3. The prefix *under-* means "lower" or "beneath." What does it mean to **underestimate** someone?

_____

_____

4. Circle *F* for fact or *O* for opinion.

A. No known cure exists for spina bifida.   F   O

B. Miller has a disability.   F   O

C. Wheelies are fun.   F   O

5. What does it mean to be **dedicated**? Write about something that you are dedicated to.

_____

_____

6. Miller wanted to send a message to the world by setting a record. Do you think that his message was heard? Why or why not?

_____

_____

■ Choose one extension activity.

A. Research other people with disabilities who have accomplished great things.

B. Write a poem about Michael Miller working hard to break this record.

A BOOMING BULLWHIP

■ Read the passage.
Whip Cracking—Longest Whip, May 24, 2006

If your parents have ever said that watching movies is a waste of time, Adam Winrich (USA) has a great argument. His interest in whips was inspired by an adventure movie that he saw when he was eight years old, *Indiana Jones and the Last Crusade*. Winrich received his first whip when he was nine. His father made it for him out of a piece of rope. At age 11, Winrich started making his own whips from techniques that he learned in the Boy Scout handbook. He has been **cracking** whips ever since.

Winrich holds seven world records for whip cracking. One of Winrich's world records involves cracking the longest whip. This whip was 216 feet (65.83 m), not including the handle. That is almost the length of a jumbo jet! It takes a lot of strength and practice to handle and crack a whip properly. But, many people do not know science is involved too.

The crack of the whip that you hear is actually something called a sonic boom. This means that the whip is traveling fast enough to break the sound barrier. On a bullwhip, the whip is thinner at the end. When the whip is snapped, sound waves begin to travel down the whip. As the waves approach the thin end, they travel faster. The loud "crack" happens as the waves pass the speed of sound.

When an object goes faster than the speed of sound, it is traveling at **supersonic** speed. Traveling at supersonic speed means that an object is going 1,125 feet per second (343 m per second). That is approximately 768 miles per hour (1,236 km per hour). This means that Winrich's whips are traveling at supersonic speed every day!

■ Answer the questions.

1. You will hear a sonic boom when an object travels fast enough to break the

   _____ .

2. What inspired Adam Winrich's interest in whips? How did he learn to make whips?

   _____

   _____

3. Which definition best describes **cracking** as it is used in this passage?
   A. breaking into pieces
   B. opening slightly
   C. making loud noises

4. To what object can the length of Winrich's whip be compared? Can you find other things that have a similar length?

   _____

   _____

5. Explain the meaning of traveling at **supersonic** speed.

   _____

   _____

■ Choose one extension activity.

A. Winrich's whip makes a sonic boom every time he cracks it. Find information about other things that make sonic booms.

B. Chuck Yeager is considered the first person to travel at supersonic speed. Find out more information about this famous American.

MAN OR GRASSHOPPER?

■ Read the passage.
Longest Somersault on Spring-Loaded Stilts, June 18, 2009

John Simkins (United Kingdom) may move like a giant grasshopper. But, he is not. He is a pro jumper. He holds the record for longest somersault on power stilts. His record-breaking somersault measured 12 feet 11 inches (4 m). John performed his somersault on a Guinness World Records TV special in China.

Simkins is 22 years old and lives in the United Kingdom. After trying on a pair of power stilts at the gym, Simkins was hooked. He has been using power stilts for two years. Now, he performs regularly in the United Kingdom and **competes** all over the world. Simkins is a member of the Pro Jump display team.

Pro jumping is the act of jumping, running, and doing tricks on power stilts. Power stilts are made with a snowboard-like foot binding and a footpad. They also contain large springs. A person can jump over three feet (1 m) high on the stilts. Some people say that it is like wearing shoes made from trampolines. A person needs good balance and **coordination** to become a good pro jumper.

DID YOU KNOW?
A German inventor named Alexander Boeck invented power stilts in 2003. Some people call the stilts *powerbocks* or *bocks* in honor of Alexander.

■ Answer the questions.

1. What is pro jumping?

_____

_____

2. Circle *T* for true or *F* for false.

A. John Simkins has been a pro jumper for over 10 years.   **T**   **F**

B. Power stilts have balls in them to make them bounce.   **T**   **F**

3. Who invented power stilts?

_____

4. The definition of **competes** is:
   A. socializes and makes new friends
   B. loses at a game
   C. races or performs against others with the goal of winning

5. What is **coordination**? What activities do you enjoy that require good coordination?

_____

_____

6. What are some of the risks to consider when attempting tricks while wearing these stilts? How could a person practice safely?

_____

_____

■ Choose one extension activity.

A. Imagine that you are a pro jumper. Write about your experience performing tricks on power stilts.

B. Power stilts were invented in 2003. Research other inventions created within the last 10 years.

BALANCING ACT

■ Read the passage.
Longest Tightrope Crossing by Bicycle, October 15, 2008

Nik Wallenda (USA) is not afraid of heights. He holds the Guinness World Records™ record for Longest Tightrope Crossing by Bicycle. He crossed a tightrope 235 feet (71 m) long and 135 feet (41 m) high.

Cameras and members of a daytime talk show watched Wallenda break the record. He rode a standard bicycle. The handlebars were removed because he did not need to steer. And, the tires were taken off so that the **bare** metal surface could fit over the tightrope. Wallenda carried a 45-foot (14-m) pole for balance.

Halfway across, he sat down and put the pole on his lap. He took out his cell phone and dialed the cohosts of the talk show. He calmly told them that it was a little windier than he thought it would be. He put the phone in his pocket and continued across.

Wallenda had one slip while he was crossing. He was **distracted** by a piece of tape on the tightrope. He said that he lost focus for a second. Fortunately, he was able to catch his balance and successfully cross to the other side.

DID YOU KNOW?
Wallenda comes from a long line of tightrope walkers. He has been training since he was four years old. During training, his parents would throw things at him while he was on the tightrope. In this way, he became prepared for any distraction.

■ Answer the questions.

1. Describe the bicycle that Nik Wallenda used to ride across the tightrope.

_____

_____

2. What did Wallenda do when he got halfway across the tightrope?

_____

_____

3. An antonym for **bare** is:
   A. covered
   B. clear
   C. exposed

4. Circle *T* for true or *F* for false.

   A. Many of Wallenda's family members are tightrope walkers.   **T**   **F**

   B. Wallenda carried a pole to give him something to focus on.   **T**   **F**

5. What does it mean when the author says that Wallenda "was **distracted** by a piece of tape"?

_____

_____

6. The passage states that Wallenda's parents would throw things at him while practicing tightrope walking to help prepare him for any distractions. Do you think this was a good idea? Do you think it worked? Why or why not?

_____

_____

■ Choose one extension activity.

A. Imagine that you are Nik Wallenda. Write a journal entry about the day that you performed the record-breaking tightrope crossing.

B. Draw a picture of Wallenda's tightrope event as the talk show hosts might have seen it.

REVIEW: GAME TIME!

■ **Match the record-holders with their imaginary nicknames.**

_____ 1. Aaron Fotheringham

_____ 2. Michael Miller

_____ 3. Ashrita Furman

_____ 4. Mark Skaife

_____ 5. Race for Life Sneaker

_____ 6. Brigham Young University students

_____ 7. Chloe Hegland

_____ 8. Adam Winrich

_____ 9. John Simkins

_____ 10. Nik Wallenda

A. Bigfoot

B. Hand-y Workers

C. Grasshopper

D. Indiana Jones

E. Lineman

F. Wheelie Popper

G. Truck Racer

H. Spoon Holder

I. The Juggler

J. Backflipper

REVIEW: GAME TIME!

■ **Find the words hidden in the puzzle. The words may be found across or down.**

athlete	juggling	promote
authentic	master	relieve
eliminations	meditate	underestimate
feat	prohibited	victor

```
a  t  h  l  e  t  e  s  m  t  y  l  m  k  j  q  u  m
u  k  i  l  o  p  j  h  n  g  b  v  f  d  c  y  r  e
t  g  y  u  i  n  v  d  s  a  a  t  r  q  u  i  l  d
h  l  p  o  i  m  n  b  v  c  k  t  y  e  r  i  f  i
e  l  i  m  i  n  a  t  i  o  n  s  u  y  b  v  c  t
n  g  f  d  c  x  s  a  w  q  y  t  k  o  j  y  g  a
t  p  r  o  h  i  b  i  t  e  d  h  n  b  v  c  b  t
i  r  n  b  g  h  u  y  u  j  k  l  o  p  b  v  c  e
c  o  l  u  n  d  e  r  e  s  t  i  m  a  t  e  v  c
d  m  b  h  n  k  l  o  p  f  n  b  n  m  u  r  t  q
p  o  l  k  m  n  g  w  q  e  a  r  t  u  j  h  g  b
v  t  j  m  n  b  s  k  m  a  s  t  e  r  k  n  m  n
i  e  o  l  k  h  g  f  d  t  o  g  f  d  s  a  w  r
l  g  d  s  i  o  o  r  q  r  t  e  v  i  c  t  o  r
k  l  j  q  w  e  t  i  o  p  s  a  b  c  v  x  o  p
l  m  h  g  r  g  h  i  h  f  v  n  u  f  d  c  n  u
h  f  d  s  p  t  q  w  s  x  c  v  u  i  l  o  q  w
j  u  g  g  l  i  n  g  h  k  i  r  e  l  i  e  v  e
```

PULLING HIS WEIGHT AND MORE!

■ Read the passage.

Heaviest Vehicle Pulled over 100 Feet—Male, September 15, 2008

Reverend Kevin Fast (Canada) does not need gas to go trucking. He does not even need an engine. He has his muscles! Reverend Fast holds the Guinness World Records™ record for the Heaviest Vehicle Pulled over 100 Feet (30.5 m). The truck weighed 126,200 pounds (57,243 kg). He used a rope to pull it 137 feet (42 m).

Reverend Fast broke the record on a live TV show. Reverend Fast did not eat before the **stunt**. He had a cup of coffee and was ready to go. Paramedics were there to keep him safe. They examined him when he finished the stunt. After the pull, Reverend Fast **exclaimed**, "I feel great!"

DID YOU KNOW?
Strongmen and strongwomen have been entertaining audiences for hundreds of years. They were a major part of the circus. Some bent metal bars. Some carried elephants or heavy cannons. Some held a cannon while it was lit and fired! They seemed to do the impossible, and crowds loved it!

Fast has pulled other massive vehicles. He recently pulled a giant airplane. It weighed 415,999 pounds (188,694 kg). Fast pulls for personal satisfaction, but he also pulls for a good cause. Reverend Fast uses his strength to help raise money for charities. It is a good way to use his talent to help others. As Fast says, "When one puts one's mind to something, it is amazing what one can achieve."

Name_____ Date_____

■ Answer the questions.

1. What did Kevin Fast use to pull the truck?

_____

2. Why were paramedics there?

_____

_____

3. What is a **stunt**? Have you ever performed a stunt? What was it?

_____

_____

4. Another word for **exclaimed** is:

    A. whispered

    B. shouted

    C. asked

5. Circle *F* for fact or *O* for opinion.

    A. A person should always have a cup of coffee before pulling heavy objects.   **F**   **0**

    B. Fast is strong enough to pull a giant airplane.   **F**   **0**

    C. Performing a stunt to raise money is not a good idea.   **F**   **0**

■ Choose one extension activity.

    A. Strongmen and strongwomen were a popular part of early circuses. Research the first circuses and find out what other performers were part of the circus.

    B. What might Kevin Fast try next? Write a dialogue you might have with him and suggest a new stunt that he should try.

PAINTING FOR PEANUTS

■ Read the passage.

**Most Expensive Painting by Elephants,
February 19, 2005**

These are not your typical artists. Watching them work would be quite a sight. Why? They are elephant artists. And, they hold a world record. They created the most expensive painting by a group of elephants. The painting is called *Cold Wind, Swirling Mist, Charming Lanna I*. It sold for $39,000.

The painting is by Kongkum, Wanpen, Kamsan, Lankam, Duanpen, Songpun, Punpetch, and Pu Ood. These eight elephants live at Maesa Elephant Camp in Thailand. It is one of several camps established to prevent the **extinction** of Asian elephants.

Only about 10 percent of the elephants in these camps become artists. They are taught to hold a paintbrush. Then, they are taught to paint on a canvas with their trunks.

The painting took them six hours to complete. It is 8 feet (2.4 m) wide and 39 feet (12 m) long. It is on two connecting panels. Panit Warin bought one of the panels. She is from Thailand and lives in California.

DID YOU KNOW?

In 1999, Richard Lair and David Soldier had an idea. They knew elephants liked listening to music. They thought that elephants might like to play music. They built giant instruments and taught the elephants to play. The Thai Elephant Orchestra has recorded two albums. They perform at the Conservation Center in Thailand.

Name_____ Date_____

■ Answer the questions.

1. Who created the record-breaking painting?

_____

_____

2. What type of surface is the painting on?

_____

_____

3. Extinction is the condition of being extinct. What animals can you think of that are extinct or are in danger of extinction?

_____

_____

4. Circle *F* for fact or *O* for opinion.

   A. Elephants are great painters.   **F**   **O**

   B. The record-breaking painting is 8 feet (2.4 m) wide and
      39 feet (12 m) long.   **F**   **O**

   C. Elephants like to listen to music.   **F**   **O**

5. Do you think that elephants like to paint? Why or why not?

_____

_____

■ Choose one extension activity.

   A. The Thai Elephant Orchestra has recorded two albums. Write titles for three new songs for them to record on their next album.

   B. If elephants can learn to paint and play giant instruments, what else do you think that they could do? Draw a picture of elephants doing something that you would like to see them do.

A RECORD WORTH SCREAMING ABOUT

■ Read the passage.

Loudest Scream, October 2000

The children in class with Jill Drake (United Kingdom) might want to carry earplugs. Drake holds the Guinness World Records™ record for loudest scream. Her scream reached 129 decibels. That is louder than the Concorde jet engine! Drake's earsplitting scream was measured in London.

Drake did not know that she had the scream in her. She discovered this unusual talent while attending a screaming competition with some of her friends. After hearing one of the screams, she joked, "I can do better than that." Her friends told her to give it a try. She went up to the microphone and let it rip. Drake could not believe it. She was amazed. "I knew I was loud, but not that loud," she said.

Drake is a classroom assistant in the United Kingdom. She says that she does not use her screaming power at school. "Believe it or not, I don't shout and scream at the children. I am very **placid** and quiet at school!" she said.

DID YOU KNOW?

The loudest noise ever recorded was a volcano erupting in Indonesia in 1883. It was on the small island of Krakatoa. Scientists estimated the sound to be around 180 decibels. That is about 13 times as loud as the sound of a jet engine from 100 feet (30 m).

Name_____ Date_____

■ Answer the questions.

1. The author writes that Jill Drake's scream is louder than a _____ .

2. How did Drake discover this talent?

_____

_____

3. An antonym for **placid** is:

    A. calm

    B. noisy

    C. cold

4. Circle *T* for true or *F* for false.

    A. Jill Drake's scream reached 180 decibels.   **T**   **F**

    B. The loudest sound ever recorded was the sound of a volcano erupting.   **T**   **F**

5. How do you think that Drake's newly discovered talent could come in handy? What would you do if you had that ability?

_____

_____

■ Choose one extension activity.

A. Find Krakatoa on a map and research the island. Is this a place where you would like to live? Why or why not?

B. If Drake's scream could be seen, what would it look like? Draw a picture of Drake's scream.

THE POLLINATOR

■ Read the passage.
Heaviest Mantle of Bees, March 9, 2009

Some of us meet bees the hard way—we get stung! But, Vipin Seth (India) does not worry much about that. He doesn't even mind all of the buzzing in his ears. That is because Seth holds the record for wearing the Heaviest **Mantle** of Bees.

Some beekeepers have hundreds or thousands of hives to care for. Often, bees will land on their keeper to stay warm. The bees remain there for long periods of time without stinging. Sometimes, the bees cover the keeper's entire body. This is called a mantle, or cloak, of bees.

Seth was covered from head to toe in bees for more than two hours. The bees weighed 136 pounds (61 kg). The mantle contained about 613,500 bees. That is one heavy human hive!

The bees used were honeybees. Honeybees can fly 15 miles (24 km) per hour. They make honey by collecting nectar from flowers. They also help plants and flowers grow by **pollinating** them.

DID YOU KNOW?
Bees dance to let their hive-mates know where to find flowers. The round dance tells other bees to look near the hive. The waggle dance shows the location of the flowers in relation to the sun.

■ Answer the questions.

1. For how long were the bees on Vipin Seth's body?

_____

2. What kind of bees were used to break the record?

_____

3. Which definition describes a **mantle** of bees?

    A. a hive full of bees

    B. a collection of nectar

    C. a covering of bees on a body

4. How do you think Seth might have prepared before beating this record? What types of things do you think he might have done to be sure he stayed safe?

_____

_____

5. What would happen to plants without bees **pollinating** them? What would be the long-term effects?

_____

_____

■ Choose one extension activity.

A. Bees use dance to communicate information. Create an expressive dance to communicate a message. Perform this dance and have classmates guess what you are trying to say.

B. What do you think that Seth was thinking while he was covered in bees? Imagine that you are Seth. Write a journal entry about your experience.

GOING TO EXTREME LENGTHS

■ **Read the passage.**

Longest Fingernails (Male)—Ever, May 30, 2009

Check out your fingernails. They probably do not **extend** very far past the tips of your fingers. Short fingernails make it easy to do everyday tasks. You can hold a pencil, open a door, or brush your teeth without your nails getting in the way. Now, imagine that your nails stretched way out in front of you. How would you do those tasks? Not as easily! Melvin Boothe (USA) from Michigan holds the record for longest male fingernails. The total length of his nails was 32.3 feet (9.85 m).

Many people have tried to grow long fingernails. The first record was held by a Chinese priest in 1955. His nails were 22 inches (56 cm) long. Lee Redmond is the record-holder for longest fingernails on a woman. She is 68 years old and from Utah. Lee went to great lengths to grow her nails. She ate a high-protein diet and soaked her fingernails in olive oil. She grew her nails for 20 years. Her record-breaking nails ended up breaking in a car accident in 2009.

Boothe took his fingernail growing very seriously. He spent most of his time in his house. He was afraid to leave because he was nervous that he might break a nail.

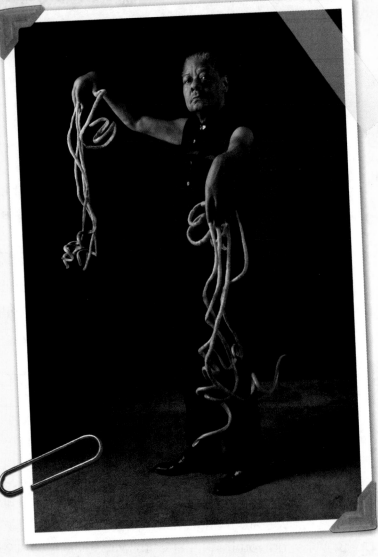

DID YOU KNOW?

Fingernails grow between one-half inch and 4 inches (1–10 cm) per year. A man's fingernails grow faster than a woman's. Fingernails generally grow faster on the hand that a person uses most often. For example, nails on the left hand grow faster on left-handed people.

■ Answer the questions.

1. What was the total length of Melvin Boothe's fingernails?

_____

2. Who set the first record for longest fingernails?

_____

3. Another word for **extend** is:
- **A.** lengthen
- **B.** shorten
- **C.** remove

4. Circle *F* for fact or *O* for opinion.

A. Many people have tried to grow long nails. **F**   **O**

B. Long nails are beautiful. **F**   **O**

C. Lee Redmond broke her fingernails in a car accident. **F**   **O**

5. The author lists some tasks that might be difficult to do with long fingernails. What other tasks do you do every day that would be difficult to do if you had fingernails like Melvin Boothe's?

_____

_____

6. Is this passage missing any important information? What additional information could the author have included?

_____

_____

■ Choose one extension activity.
- **A.** Find out ways that people can keep their fingernails healthy. Then, write a five-item list of dos and don'ts.
- **B.** Draw a picture of yourself sporting extra-long fingernails. How would they be shaped or decorated?

A WAIST THAT'S LACED

■ Read the passage.
Smallest Waist—Living Person, 1999

Cathie Jung (USA) cannot buy a pair of jeans at the mall. They will not have her size. Jung holds the Guinness World Records™ record for Smallest Waist. Her waist is the size of a large mayonnaise jar! It measures 15 inches (38 cm).

How did Jung get her tiny waist? She wears corsets. A corset is an undergarment that fits tightly around the waist and chest. Long ago, it was fashionable for ladies to have a **slender** waist. So, many women wore corsets. Some men and women wear corsets today to help them support a weak or injured back.

Corsets often have laces, so they can be pulled very tightly. Think about pulling the laces of your tennis shoe tight enough to squeeze your foot. This is how a corset works around the waist.

Jung has been wearing corsets every day for the past 12 years. She **rarely** goes without a corset. She removes it only to shower. She has about 100 corsets. She even has a swimsuit with a corset sewn into it.

Jung is 70 years old and from North Carolina. She is married with three children. Jung often has difficulty sitting in low chairs. Sometimes she must sit on raised chairs at restaurants to be comfortable. She says that she is happy eating small meals and can do almost everything normally.

■ Answer the questions.

1. Why can't Cathie Jung buy jeans at the mall?

_____

_____

2. What does the author compare Jung's waist to?

_____

3. Something that is **slender** can also be described as:
   A. big
   B. thin
   C. thick

4. Circle *F* for fact or *O* for opinion.

   A. Jung's waist looks fine.   F   O

   B. Jung wears a corset almost 24 hours a day.   F   O

   C. Jung has three children.   F   O

5. **Rarely**, as used in the passage, means:
   A. highly valued
   B. lightly cooked
   C. hardly ever

6. Jung says that she can do most things normally except for sitting in low chairs. What activities do you think would be difficult for you if you wore a corset all day?

_____

_____

■ Choose one statement. Then, explain why you agree or disagree.

A. Corsets should be worn only by people with back problems.

B. People should not do extreme things to change their appearance.

SPEEDY SOFA

■ Read the passage.
Fastest Furniture, May 11, 2007

This couch has no place in a living room. It was made for the road! Edward China created the speedy sofa. It holds the Guinness World Records™ record for Fastest Furniture. Marek Turowski (United Kingdom) is the couch potato who won the opportunity to drive the sofa. It went 92 miles (148 km) per hour.

Turowski is 38 years old. He is a gardener and lives in London. An online auction was held for the chance to drive the sofa. Turowski won the auction. The money raised from the auction went to a foundation for medical research.

Edward China, also known as Edd, is 35 years old and has built many **extraordinary** vehicles. He has made a moving garden shed, a moving bathroom, and an alien spacecraft. He started a business that rents out some of the vehicles. A bed called the Street Sleeper is a popular item.

Edd China has broken other records. He built the largest motorized shopping cart. The cart is 12 feet (3.5 m) tall. He also built the world's Fastest Office. The office included a desk, four chairs, a computer, and a water cooler. It reached a speed of 87 miles (140 km) per hour.

■ Answer the questions.

1. How did Marek Turowski get to drive the motorized sofa?

_____

_____

2. What other vehicles has Edd China built?

_____

_____

3. The prefix *extra-* means "beyond" or "in addition to." What is probably the definition of **extraordinary**?

_____

_____

4. Circle *T* for true or *F* for false.

A. Marek Turowski invented the speedy sofa.   **T**   **F**

B. Edd China has built only one record-breaking vehicle.   **T**   **F**

5. What do you think it would be like to take the sofa out for a drive? How do you think people driving cars would react to the sofa?

_____

_____

■ Choose one extension activity.

A. Write a song about what it must have been like for Marek Turowski to drive the record-breaking sofa.

B. Imagine that you are Edd China. What would you like to put on the road? Design and draw your own interesting motorized vehicle.

RECORD-BREAKING BOWL BREAKER

■ **Read the passage.**

Most Bowls Broken with One Finger in One Minute, April 11, 2009

Fan Weipeng (China) has one powerful finger. He used it to break 102 bowls. Weipeng holds the Guinness World Records™ record for Most Bowls Broken with One Finger in One Minute.

Weipeng lives in China. He studied martial arts with the Shaolin School. Strength is not the only skill that Weipeng needed to achieve his goal of setting the record. He needed great focus and **concentration** too. Weipeng uses what he has learned to do unbelievable things. He even can support his whole body using only two fingers. Imagine what he can do with his whole hand!

Weipeng's talents have taken him far. He was a performer in the opening ceremony for the Beijing Olympic Games in 2008. He worked very hard to prepare for that event. The training process was **intense**. The performers trained for over a year. Weipeng said that once they trained for 48 hours. "We trained until three in the morning and fell asleep in the audience seats. When we woke up, we continued—we trained for two days and two nights," said Weipeng.

DID YOU KNOW?

Shaolin is a type of martial arts. It began around the year 1600. Legend says that Shaolin taught people how to do amazing things. They were able to do things like punch through concrete walls and walk on water.

■ **Answer the questions.**

1. What are Vittorio Innocente's two passions?

_____

_____

2. Who set the previous Guinness World Record for Deepest Cycling Underwater?

_____

3. The prefix *sub-* means "under," "at a lower level," or "of a lesser quality." What does **submerged** mean? Name two words that contain the same prefix.

_____

_____

4. Circle *F* for fact or *O* for opinion.

   A. Innocente is amazing.   **F**   **O**

   B. Innocente is Italian.   **F**   **O**

   C. Innocente raises money for cancer research.   **F**   **O**

5. An antonym for **remarkable** is:

   A. ordinary

   B. fast

   C. unbelievable

6. What is the message that Innocente is trying to send to the world? Do you think that he is accomplishing that? Why or why not?

_____

_____

■ **Choose one extension activity.**

A. Draw a comic strip showing fish and other sea creatures watching Innocente riding by. Write the cartoon animals' conversation.

B. Write the words to a song that Mark Gottlieb might play underwater.

SPREADING THE WORD

■ Read the passage.

Most Children Reading with an Adult (Multiple Venue), September 20, 2007

What would it sound like if 200,000 people were reading at the same time? Not very loud for this world record, because these people were scattered all over the world. A total of 238,620 children and adults read the same book on the same day to set a world record. Preschool children all over the world read *The Story of Ferdinand* by Munro Leaf. The event was called Read for the Record.

Read for the Record was created by Jumpstart. Jumpstart is a **nonprofit** organization. A nonprofit organization is a charity. It uses its money to do good things. Two college students started Jumpstart in 1993. They wanted to help preschool children. Members of Jumpstart volunteer their time. Each member is matched with a preschool student for the year. The goal is to help children learn to read. Since Jumpstart began, it has **assisted** over 70,000 preschool children.

DID YOU KNOW?

March 2 is the birthday of a beloved author of children's books. Born Theodor Geisel, he is best known to children, parents, and teachers as Dr. Seuss. Each year on Dr. Seuss's birthday, many classrooms and homes across the U.S. celebrate Read Across America Day. Schools, libraries, and community centers promote book reading, organize book fairs, and read aloud to groups of people.

GUINNESS WORLD RECORDS

■ Answer the questions.

1. What book was read to break the record?

_____

2. Who created the event?

_____

3. A person who is **assisted** is:

    A. asked an opinion

    B. given help

    C. being tested

4. Circle *F* for fact or *O* for opinion.

    A. The goal of Jumpstart is to help children learn to read.   **F**   **O**

    B. Jumpstart has good ideas.   **F**   **O**

    C. Reading is fun.   **F**   **O**

5. The prefix *non-* means "not." What is a **nonprofit** organization?

_____

_____

6. If you could start your own nonprofit organization, who or what would your organization help?

_____

_____

■ Choose one extension activity.

A. Imagine that you are asked to create a magazine advertisement for Read for the Record. Draw a picture of your ad.

B. Jumpstart is a nonprofit organization that was started by two students. Research other nonprofit organizations that were started by students.

REVIEW: WILD, WACKY & WEIRD

■ **Read each clue. Then, unscramble each set of letters to find a synonym. Write the synonym on the line.**

1. lengthen _____ T E X N E D

2. amazing _____ R A M B L E A R K E

3. helped _____ D E S I T S A S

4. cloak _____ T A M E L N

5. infrequently _____ Y E A R L R

6. underwater _____ G E R M S B U D E

7. peaceful _____ A C I D L P

8. thin _____ R E L S E N D

9. focus _____ T R A C E C O T I N N N O

10. shouted _____ M E X I C A D E L

REVIEW: WILD, WACKY & WEIRD

■ **Match the record-holders with their imaginary job titles.**

_____ **1.** Wanpen

A. furniture mover

_____ **2.** Fan Weipeng

B. waist watcher

_____ **3.** Marek Turowski

C. nail measurer

_____ **4.** Vipin Seth

D. cloak wearer

_____ **5.** Cathie Jung

E. London screamer

_____ **6.** Vittorio Innocente

F. famous painter

_____ **7.** Kevin Fast

G. stuntman reverend

_____ **8.** Jill Drake

H. bowl breaker

_____ **9.** Edd China

I. passionate pedal pusher

_____ **10.** Melvin Boothe

J. rooms-that-go designer

ANSWER KEY

Page 11
1. New Year's Eve party; 2. C;
3. Answers will vary but may include dog food and department store commercials, national morning show.
4. Jack Russell terriers are intelligent, athletic, and fun-loving. 5. Answers will vary. 6. Answers will vary.

Page 13
1. Komodo monitors or ora; 2. F, F;
3. C; 4. B; 5. Answers will vary. 6. A

Page 15
1. three to four miles (4.8–6.4 km);
2. A prehensile tail is used for grabbing things and commonly used by animals for balance. Answers will vary. 3. C; 4. An herbivore is an animal whose diet is made up mostly of plants, leaves, fruit, and flowers. Answers will vary. 5. Answers will vary but may include they are loud and sleep most of the day. 6. Answers will vary.

Page 17
1. F, T; 2. C; 3. B; 4. Answers will vary but may include swim, can be different colors, use camouflage, and have fins. 5. Answers will vary but may include they mate for life, the males give birth to fully formed young, and they swim upright. 6. A dorsal fin is on the back and pectoral fins are on the sides.

Page 19
1. B; 2. Africa; 3. A; 4. Lurch's horns were growing faster than expected. His horns were unusually large in circumference. 5. dogs, cats, geese, donkeys, zebra, deer, and water buffalo

Page 21
1. C; 2. because they live in total darkness; 3. Answers will vary.
4. A; 5. When this mole is looking for food, its nose tentacles are constantly moving. When a mole eats, the tentacles are clumped together and stay out of the way. 6. B

Page 23
1. 11 or 12, three; 2. Their environment is very colorful. 3. B; 4. Answers will vary. 5. T, T

Page 25
1. C; 2. B; 3. A; 4. because they brought back or "retrieved" what the hunters had caught; 5. to keep from going into something, Answers will vary. 6. Answers will vary.

Page 27
1. T, T; 2. C; 3. Answers will vary. 4. A;
5. B

Page 29
1. tarantula; 2. originally from, Answers will vary. 3. C; 4. A;
5. Answers will vary. 6. B

Page 31
1. F, F; 2. A; 3. affected by, Answers will vary. 4. Answers will vary.
5. Answers will vary.

Page 33
1. T, F; 2. When a boy showed him the current record, he realized that his goat could beat it. 3. B; 4. Answers will vary. 5. "I thought it might be nice if Uncle Sam were displayed somewhere that people could see him." "Uncle Sam could beat that."
6. Answers will vary.

Page 34
1. balloon; 2. tennis; 3. balls;
4. howler; 5. sea; 6. horse;
7. star-nosed; 8. mole; 9. Mantis;
10. shrimp; 11. lizard; 12. steer;
13. Goliath; 14. bird-eating; 15. pigmy;
16. rattlesnake

Page 35

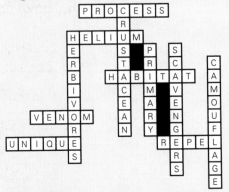

Page 37
1. F, T; 2. hands and feet; 3. Answers will vary but may include that Campo hired the boys and taught them skills so that they could live dignified lives.
4. B; 5. Answers will vary. 6. Answers will vary. 7. Answers will vary.

Page 39
1. the engine from a tank; 2. C;
3. a seat attached to the side of a motorcycle; 4. Answers will vary.
5. F, F

Page 41
1. Alberta, Canada; 2. 14; 3. "the eighth wonder of the world"; 4. C;
5. providing enjoyment or entertainment, Answers will vary.
6. B

Page 43
1. T, T; 2. He can fit himself through the opening of a tennis racket with its strings removed. 3. the midsection of the body, Answers will vary. 4. C;
5. Answers will vary. 6. Answers will vary.

Page 45
1. digging for coal or minerals near the surface of the ground instead of deep underground; 2. F, F; 3. B; 4. Answers will vary. 5. No, Answers will vary.

Page 47
1. 8, 281.5, 127.7; 2. C; 3. C;
4. Answers will vary. 5. Answers will vary.

Page 49
1. to show that solar power is the perfect choice for boats and to raise awareness about cleaner energy;
2. F, T; 3. A; 4. A; 5. O, F, F

Page 51
1. F, T; 2. C; 3. A; 4. because he cannot wear normal-sized clothes;
5. They have given him medication to stop his growth.

Page 53
1. C; 2. putting a snake into his nose and pulling it out of his mouth; 3. B;
4. because they are flexible; 5. A snake got stuck in his throat. He could bite the snake or the snake would bite him. 6. A; 7. a nutrient found in foods, needed to build strong muscles

Page 54
1. G; 2. A; 3. C; 4. E; 5. H; 6. I; 7. D;
8. F; 9. J; 10. B

Page 55
1. sidecar; 2. crest; 3. amusement;
4. torso; 5. excavator; 6. factory;
7. absorb; 8. ship; 9. stumped;
10. food

Page 57
1. F, T; 2. home of the snow; 3. correct, Answers will vary. 4. India was part of Africa, and the Himalayas did not exist. 5. Answers will vary.

Page 59
1. 1,000, vegetable; 2. A; 3. C; 4. he grew the world's heaviest onion, at the Harrogate Flower Show in United Kingdom; 5. yearly; 6. T, T

Page 61
1. F, T; 2. a geode that is completely filled with crystals; 3. from bubbles trapped in volcanic rock, millions of years; 4. a purple gemstone, jewelry; 5. C

Page 63
1. 3,000; 2. hair oil, food; 3. A; 4. Alike: Both are a source of vitamins and minerals, Different: Black seeds are used for making oil and striped seeds are used as food. 5. Answers will vary. 6. F, O, O

Page 65
1. C; 2. good, loose soil, sunshine, lots of water, plenty of space; 3. A; 4. Answers will vary. 5. Answers will vary.

Page 67
1. F, F; 2. Borneo; 3. A; 4. able to be accessed or reached, Answers will vary. 5. Answers will vary. 6. Answers will vary. 7. Answers will vary.

Page 69
1. north; 2. F, T; 3. B; 4. a place to stay; 5. Answers will vary. 6. Answers will vary.

Page 71
1. 520; 2. an activity done just for fun, Answers will vary. 3. A; 4. Answers will vary. 5. Answers will vary. 6. Answers will vary.

Page 73
1. B; 2. T, T; 3. C; 4. something that keeps you warm, Answers will vary. 5. Answers will vary. 6. Answers will vary.

Page 75
1. 271 feet (82.6 m), four million; 2. B; 3. B; 4. temperature changes, hard ground, lack of water, people. 5. Answers will vary.

Page 76
1. Himalayan; 2. iron; 3. road; 4. fossil; 5. Geode; 6. Sequoia; 7. Mexico; 8. cucumbers; 9. sand; 10. castles; 11. ice; 12. IceHotel; 13. Onion

Page 77
nodule; quartz; recipes; intricate; harvest; fossil; source; estimated; exhibit; pastime; accurate; originated; embedded; accessible; EARTH IS EXTREME!

Page 79
1. He watched his older brother skate. 2. B; 3. A; 4. F, F; 5. a person who is skilled in sports or in other physical activities, Answers will vary. 6. Answers will vary.

Page 81
1. A; 2. T, F; 3. to reduce or to make less severe, Answers will vary. 4. A; 5. Answers will vary. 6. Answers will vary.

Page 83
1. T, T; 2. He set the record for fastest mile covered while bouncing a kangaroo ball (or hoppity hop). 3. an accomplishment, Answers will vary. 4. C; 5. Answers will vary.

Page 85
1. an Australian race car driver; 2. a truck that a car company makes a large number of; 3. 168.7 miles (271.4 km) per hour; 4. O, O, F; 5. A; 6. Answers will vary.

Page 87
1. F, T; 2. 87 feet (27 m); 3. A; 4. to advertise, Answers will vary. 5. Answers will vary. 6. Answers will vary.

Page 89
1. A; 2. B; 3. people leaving a game when they lose; 4. the winner in a competition, Answers will vary. 5. Answers will vary.

Page 91
1. keeping the ball in the air by bouncing it off a player's feet, legs, and head; 2. 16; 3. C; 4. T, F; 5. Answers will vary. 6. Answers will vary. 7. Answers will vary.

Page 93
1. engineering students at Delft University of Technology in the Netherlands; 2. It has two wheels like most bikes. 3. C; 4. O, F, O; 5. the science of designing and building things; 6. Answers will vary.

Page 95
1. the Longest Wheelie in a Wheelchair; 2. ride on the back wheels; 3. to think that someone or something is less than they are, Answers will vary. 4. F, F, O; 5. to work very hard toward a particular task or purpose, Answers will vary. 6. Answers will vary.

Page 97
1. sound barrier; 2. the movie *Indiana Jones and the Last Crusade*, the Boy Scout handbook; 3. C; 4. a jumbo jet, Answers will vary. 5. going faster than the speed of sound

Page 99
1. the act of jumping, running, and doing tricks on power stilts; 2. F, F; 3. Alexander Boeck; 4. C; 5. the ability to control and move your body in a skilled way, Answers will vary. 6. Answers will vary.

Page 101
1. a standard bicycle with the handlebars and tires removed; 2. He stopped, sat down, pulled out his cell phone, and made a call. 3. A; 4. T, F; 5. He lost focus for a second. 6. Answers will vary.

Page 102
1. J; 2. F; 3. H; 4. G; 5. A; 6. B; 7. I; 8. D; 9. C; 10. E

Page 103

Page 105
1. his muscles and a rope; 2. to make sure that Fast stayed safe and to examine him afterward; 3. an amazing trick or accomplishment, Answers will vary. 4. B; 5. O, F, O

Page 107
1. Eight elephants from the Maesa Elephant Camp in Thailand: Kongkum, Wanpen, Kamsan, Lankam, Duanpen, Songpun, Punpetch, and Pu Ood; 2. two connecting panels of canvas; 3. Answers will vary. 4. O, F, F; 5. Answers will vary.

Page 109
1. Concorde jet engine; 2. She was attending a screaming competition with friends. 3. B; 4. F, T; 5. Answers will vary.

Page 111
1. more than two hours; 2. honeybees; 3. C; 4. Answers will vary. 5. Answers will vary.

Page 113

1. 32.3 feet (9.85 m); 2. a Chinese priest; 3. A; 4. F, O, F; 5. Answers will vary. 6. Answers will vary.

Page 115

1. They do not have her size. 2. a large jar of mayonnaise; 3. B; 4. O, F, F; 5. C; 6. Answers will vary.

Page 117

1. He won the chance in an online auction. 2. a moving garden shed, bathroom, alien spacecraft, bed, shopping cart, office; 3. beyond the ordinary; 4. F, F; 5. Answers will vary.

Page 119

1. Most Bowls Broken with One Finger in One Minute; 2. support his whole body; 3. B; 4. T, F; 5. B; 6. People could punch through concrete walls and walk on water. Answers will vary.

Page 121

1. cycling and scuba diving; 2. Vittorio Innocente; 3. underwater, Answers will vary. 4. O, F, F; 5. A; 6. that mountain bikes can go anywhere, Answers will vary.

Page 123

1. *The Story of Ferdinand*; 2. Jumpstart; 3. B; 4. F, O, O; 5. an organization that does not make a profit; 6. Answers will vary.

Page 124

1. extend; 2. remarkable; 3. assisted; 4. mantle; 5. rarely; 6. submerged; 7. placid; 8. slender; 9. concentration; 10. exclaimed

Page 125

1. F; 2. H; 3. A; 4. D; 5. B; 6. I; 7. G; 8. E; 9. J; 10. C